12 ESSENTIAL SKILLS FOR SOFTWARE ARCHITECTS

12 ESSENTIAL SKILLS FOR SOFTWARE ARCHITECTS

DAVE HENDRICKSEN

Karen,
I really appreciate
your positive approach
to solving problems!
Dave

♦♦Addison-Wesley

Upper Saddle River, NJ • Boston • Indianapolis • San Francisco
New York • Toronto • Montreal • London • Munich • Paris • Madrid
Capetown • Sydney • Tokyo • Singapore • Mexico City

The publisher offers excellent discounts on this book when ordered in quantity for bulk purchases or special sales, which may include electronic versions and/or custom covers and content particular to your business, training goals, marketing focus, and branding interests. For more information, please contact:

U.S. Corporate and Government Sales
(800) 382-3419
corpsales@pearsontechgroup.com

For sales outside the United States please contact:

International Sales
international@pearson.com

Visit us on the Web: informit.com/aw

Library of Congress Cataloging-in-Publication Data

Hendricksen, Dave, 1964–
   12 essential skills for software architects / Dave Hendricksen.
       p.   cm.
   Includes bibliographical references and index.
   ISBN 978-0-321-71729-0 (pbk. : alk. paper)
 1. Computer software developers—Vocational guidance. 2. Computer software developers—Life skills guides. 3. Computer software developers—Professional relationships.
4. Career development. I. Title. II. Title: Twelve essential skills for software architects.
   QA76.25.H47 2011
   005.1092—dc23

                                                2011027673

ISBN-13: 978-0-321-71729-0
ISBN-10:   0-321-71729-5
Text printed in the United States on recycled paper at RR Donnelley in Crawfordsville, Indiana.
First printing, September 2011

To my wife, Jennifer, my son, Tim, and my daughter, Katie.

CONTENTS

Part III Business Skills 175

PREFACE

The soft stuff is always harder than the hard stuff.

—Roger Enrico, Vice Chairman, Pepsico

As you start reading this book, I hope you are prepared to keep an open mind and are willing to try some new approaches to your daily life.

My name is Dave Hendricksen, and I have the privilege of being a software architect for Thomson Reuters, where the focus of my work is on producing intelligent legal information. This includes everything from data capture to data display of legislative, regulatory, and intellectual property materials on Westlaw.com. I have been married for 22 years to a beautiful lady. We have two great kids, one cat, one dog, and a koi pond.

As a technology person, I have always considered myself to be slightly different from the rest of the "normal" world. Thinking analytically, focusing on problem solving, building things, and gaming for hours on end all come quite naturally to me. I love to learn new things. For me, going to school has always been great fun; I have a bachelor's degree in math and Bible and two master's degrees (one in computer science and one in the management of technology).

I love to work hard and am willing to put in whatever amount of effort is needed to get a project done on time. I love to hear my boss say, "Great job, Dave." Of course, my thinking would be this: Do great work, get promoted, and life is awesome—and to a degree, this has been true, at least up to the point where technology enters management. An invisible ether exists here that prevents a large number of talented individuals from moving up the organizational hierarchy and any further in their careers. This magical ether detects a lack of soft skills and quietly prevents these individuals from advancing to the next rungs of the ladder.

My goal for this book is to enable you to learn the essential soft skills that you will need to master as a software architect.

This book assumes that you already have the requisite technical skills to become an architect; as such, it does not focus on these types of skills. Instead, this book focuses on 12 essential soft skills that are critical to the daily activities of being an architect. These are the skills that are typically the most challenging for people with technology backgrounds.

The 12 skills in this book are organized into three groups: relationship skills, personal skills, and business skills. These classifications are based on the notion of relative priority; that is, if you don't have relationship skills, the other two areas don't matter. You are not likely to be promoted to the position of architect or to stay in the role of architect for long if you do not relate to people and various parts of your organization well. Similarly, if you don't have the necessary personal skills, business skills will not be deemed as important. In the end, all of these areas are important, but from a prioritization perspective, if you don't have the foundation skills of relationships mastered first, working on business skills will not have the impact that you are likely looking for.

I view this as a pyramid of skills, which is depicted in Figure Pref-1.

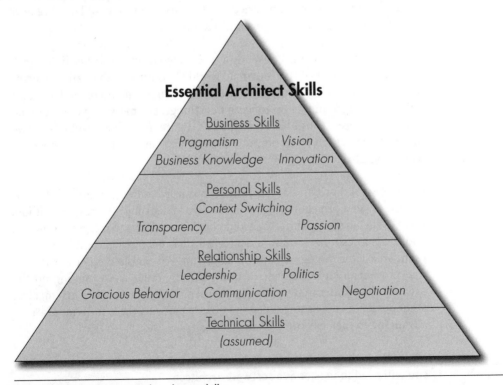

Figure Pref-1   Essential architect skills

I hope you enjoy reading this book and learn some new things that will enable you to become an architect, improve your skills as an architect, or better understand the nature and role of an architect. If you have any questions or comments, feel free to email me at dave@hendricksen.org.

Have great day!

Dave

ACKNOWLEDGMENTS

I want to thank the very helpful staff at Addison-Wesley—specifically, Raina Chrobak, Sheri Cain, Anna Popick, Chris Guzikowski, and freelance copy editor Jill Hobbs. They have been absolutely terrific in helping me work on my first book.

I want to thank my boss at Thomson Reuters, Mick Atton, for all his mentoring and for reviewing this book.

In addition, I want to thank Brad Appleton, Bob Maksimchuk, and Davie Sweis for their insights and detailed reviews of this book. I would also like to say thank you to Colin Renouf for his very detailed review of this book and for the knowledge of psychology that he shared with me. I also want to thank my wife, Jennifer, and my son, Tim, for taking time to review the book.

Finally, I want to thank my family and parents for their patience and support while I completed this book.

ABOUT THE AUTHOR

Dave Hendricken is a software architect for Thomson Reuters.

Dave enjoys working closely with new product development teams to create innovative legal products for large-scale online platforms such as Westlaw.com.

In his spare time, Dave enjoys mentoring the Eagan High School Robotics team, downhill skiing with his kids, fishing for large-mouth bass, golfing early in the morning, and spending time at the cabin building things like trebuchets, go-carts, and rain barrel watering systems with his kids.

PART I

RELATIONSHIP SKILLS

Technology does not run an enterprise; relationships do.

—Patricia Fripp

The most important single ingredient in the formula of success is knowing how to get along with people.

—Theodore Roosevelt, U.S. President

I am convinced that nothing we do is more important than hiring and developing people. At the end of the day you bet on people, not on strategies.

—Larry Bossidy, CEO of Allied Signal

If you wish to make a man your enemy, tell him simply, "You are wrong." This method works every time.

—Henry C. Link

The real art of conversation is not only to say the right thing in the right place, but to leave unsaid the wrong thing at the tempting moment.

—Lady Dorothy Nevill, English Writer

This first part of the book focuses on the five essential relationship skills for an architect. Specifically, Chapters 1 through 5 focus on principles, strategies, and other areas such as interacting with executives that will help you become more effective in managing your architectural relationships:

- **Chapter 1: Gracious Behavior.** Your ability to be gracious with others in all circumstances.
- **Chapter 2: Communication.** Your ability to effectively interact with others.
- **Chapter 3: Negotiation.** Your ability to get things done.

- **Chapter 4: Leadership.** Your ability to influence what and how things get done.
- **Chapter 5: Politics.** Your ability to interact in a political marketplace.

Relationship skills are the foundational layer of the soft skills needed to be an architect (see Figure P1-1).

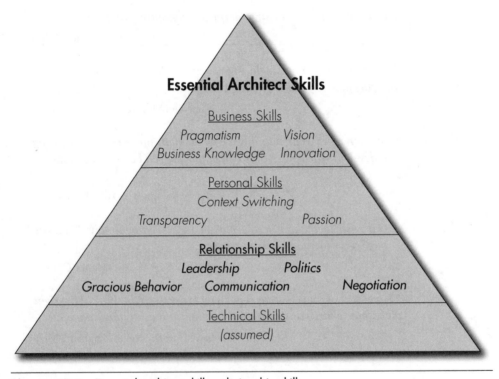

Figure P1-1   Essential architect skills: relationship skills

Chapter 1

Gracious Behavior

Behavior is a mirror in which every one displays his own image.

—Johann Wolfgang von Goethe

The true test of character is not how much we know how to do, but how we behave when we don't know what to do.

—John W. Holt, Jr.

Act the way you'd like to be and soon you'll be the way you act.

—George W. Crane

Working as an architect requires you to interact with a wide range of individuals throughout an organization. To be truly successful in this position, you need the best ideas and thoughts from everyone you encounter. One of the best ways to engage everyone (even those people whom you don't agree with or even necessarily get along with) is to be gracious and professional in all circumstances.

Gracious behavior is a strong tenant of FIRST Robotics (an organization that is dedicated to inspiring young people to become science and technology leaders). Gracious behavior is the notion of doing one's work both graciously and professionally.

This chapter unveils one of the key essential soft skills needed by a software architect—being gracious in all circumstances.

How Would Others Describe You?

If I were to run into some people who know you (your neighbors, coworkers, family, and so on), how would they describe you?

- Would they say you are hard-working?
- Would they say you have integrity?

- Would they say you are gracious?
- Or would they go into a long list of soft-skill challenges, all confirming that you are, well, a typical technical person—great in the technical arena, but not so much when it comes to soft skills?

THE TECHNICAL CEILING

One of the challenges that the very best technology folks (the gurus—the ones you go to when you have a difficult problem that must be solved and solved right) often have is that they are often a complete pain to deal with. Their approach and means of interacting are completely focused on correctness to the minutest detail. Does this description sound familiar?

Often, you can barely get through a conversation without these individuals issuing a play-by-play analysis of the minor variations of incorrectness being conveyed. By the time you are done explaining the problem, you are tired.

When they come back and the problem is solved with an elegant solution, the customer is thrilled. But the next time you need to ask them to do something, you always weigh the personal costs you need to endure to get the solution. You think to yourself, "Is it truly worth it?"

When review time rolls around, these technology mavens receive stellar comments about the great work they have done. The feedback about their poor soft skills is usually overlooked or perhaps mentioned as a small comment. Year after year, reinforcement is given that the way they approach their work is excellent. Unfortunately, the technical barrier to their advancement within the organization is often growing thicker.

As time progresses and an individual in this situation seeks a promotion, he or she faces several challenges. One key challenge is that senior management does not care to be critiqued by someone located below them on the organization chart. As a consequence, the managers and directors between this individual and the executive are unlikely to want to be associated with the negative repercussions of exposing this person to an executive.

The problem for the technology person—who is clearly talented—is that he or she needs an executive sponsor to move up in the organization. If the manager or director decides to take a chance and bring the "talented" individual to a meeting and the executive gets "roasted," the executive's first impression of the person will be negative; it will take years for that person to overcome the first bad impression, and the manager will be really sorry that he or she took this chance and will likely not want a repeat of this event. In turn, the ceiling for the talented technology individual continues to thicken (see Figure 1-1).

For some in the technical ranks, such a disaster also sets them on the path of perception that the technically untalented move into management. In some sense, this notion has the ring of truth, although there is more involved than simply that the socially enabled are able to advance into management. Specially, these individuals' skill sets are more geared toward relating to other people and communication.

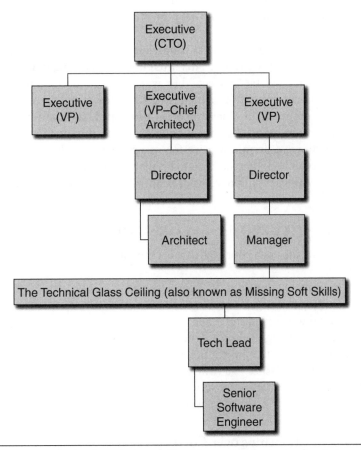

Figure 1-1   The "technical glass ceiling" in most cases is simply missing soft skills. These skills can be learned, although in most cases, the missing knowledge is usually filled in through a focused effort to change.

For people filling more senior positions, detailed technical skills are useful, but the balance begins to shift toward their ability to successfully interact with others, to get things done, and to sell their viewpoint. From technologists' point of view, the simple fact that the solution they are bringing forward is technically pure should be sufficient to win its acceptance. They often believe that the solution should stand on its own without any sales required, and that everyone should simply admire the beauty of the solution.

Sometimes a technical person will fail to perceive that for any project, a wide range of factors need to be taken into account. In many cases, the solution itself likely needs to be just good enough to meet the needs and requirements of the users; it does not need to be gold plated (although it is technically fun to refine and re-refine perfection).

The product needs to deliver the best possible return on investment (ROI) to those who are footing the bill. This often means squeezing in more functionality that may not be "perfect," but is, in fact, good enough at a cost that enables enough money to be made and in a time frame to meet market needs. Often competing products are being developed, and the organization needs to be first to market to gain the market leadership position that will enable it to charge a premium price for its product. At other times, other factors may come into play, such as in a replatforming project where maintaining quality and keeping costs under control are the primary drivers.

THE ROAD TO BECOMING A GRACIOUS PROFESSIONAL

The road to gracious behavior begins with the following steps:

- Choosing relationships over correctness
- Learning to delegate
- Realizing that life is reflexive
- Acting as though words are seeds
- Dealing with others with integrity and honesty without bluntness
- Confronting issues in a timely manner
- Providing a professional service
- Forgiving and forgetting past offenses

Choosing Relationships over Correctness

One of the first principles to learn in becoming a gracious professional is to choose relationships over correctness.

In the world of business, relationships are everything. They determine which projects or jobs you have access to. They also determine how motivated individuals are to work on your "high priority" project.

So often in our daily experience, we are driven to make our voice heard, and we operate from the position that our thoughts, plans, designs, methods, facts, and assumptions are correct. Often in the middle of conversations, we hear things that we perceive to be incorrect and feel the great urge to correct this misstatement. When it comes to sharing our "corrections," as one reviewer put it, "Waiting is wisdom."

From a software development and engineering perspective, we are trained to look for defects (imperfections) and to remove these flaws quickly (we have all kinds of ways to deal with this task—pair programming, unit tests, functional tests, stress tests, code reviews, and so on). The challenge lies in the indisputable fact that people are not software: We don't need to drive out their imperfections (in most cases, our perception of their imperfections may be figments of our imagination).

Ask yourself these questions:

- Does making this correction matter?
- Will it cost the company significantly if I don't speak up?

The odds are that the answers to both questions will be no. Your best option is often to keep quiet, even if you are right. The challenge is to seek to maintain integrity and authenticity with others, to provide valuable insights when appropriate, and to offer opportunities for others to learn in a relatively quiet manner. Your best guide is to have other people's best interests at heart and to use your best judgment to figure out how to proceed.

In my own work, I have found that valuing relationships over "correctness"— my own limited view of the world—enables me to naturally start out in an environment that fosters collaboration (see Figure 1-2). It naturally puts me into a mode that draws me into listening to what others are saying, and being willing to put my assumptions on the table as being mutable, because building the relationship is more important than being correct.

The result is that a conversation begins and synergy is able to blossom. This environment encourages the best ideas to be brought forward, to be examined, and to be potentially rejected and reformulated into a new and

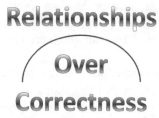

Relationships

Over

Correctness

Figure 1-2   Choose relationships over correctness: People are more
important.

improved concept that is simply better than any of the individual contribu-
tors (including myself) would have ever imagined independently.

Once people believe that you are putting your ideas at risk and are willing to allow others to freely improve an idea, they will step up to the table
and begin taking joint ownership. At this critical moment, it has suddenly
become safe for your partners to begin contributing their best ideas.

The reverse is also true. If you are, in fact, not open to allowing your golden
idea to be modified in any way, you are putting up fences that loudly declare
to others that they should stand back: Greatness has been presented to you.
Please admire, but don't touch—it's a bit like being at a museum. One key
consideration to keep in mind is that there is a fine line between elegant
correctness and responsibility; remember that beauty lies in the eye of the
beholder.

The environment you should be looking for is more like a shared garden
where ideas are free to blossom and weeds are allowed to be removed. By
taking this approach, you begin to see the value that others bring to the
table. Their unique perspectives are able to whittle away at an idea's weaknesses that may have been imperceptible to you, as the developer. In all too
many cases, our own view of the world simply blinds us to the potential
faults in our proposed solutions.

At a certain point, a direction needs to be chosen. At that point, everyone
needs to get on board and respect the decision that is made, even if it is not
the one they would have chosen.

There are nearly always improvements to an idea floating around that are
not in the developer's own cognitive universe. I am constantly amazed at

the sheer volume of ideas that every person possesses and is willing to share when that individual feels he or she is in a safe environment.

Everyone loves to talk and have their ideas be added into the ecosystem. Once your coworkers are willing to contribute, they will begin taking ownership and will be willing to contribute even more ideas. Normally, the first few ideas that people throw out are "safe" ideas. They are testing the waters to see if sharks are present. If it proves to be safe, they are willing to begin bringing out their best and brightest ideas.

I have been amazed at how what initially appears to be a weak idea can grow to become a key factor that strengthens a concept. It is the multidimensional nature of the solution that builds strength. When you think of a piece of fabricated lumber, it is not the individual layers that are responsible for its strength; rather, binding them together makes the board strong.

> **Note**
>
> From past observations, one of the leading causes of someone getting fired is poor relationships. In a very real sense, it is in your best interest to learn to build relationships by choosing to value relationships over correctness.

When you focus on relationships over correctness, you will naturally engage in building and maintaining a strong professional network that will enable you to capitalize on future opportunities and maintain a margin of safety when times get tough.

Learning to Delegate

As you progress in your career and fill more leadership positions, you must inevitably allow others to take over and bring a portion of a project to completion.

A key concept that enables this evolution to occur is allowing others to help determine the solution. If the individual has been allowed to contribute to the idea, a sense of ownership will already be in place that will allow the person to literally take the project and run with it. In a real sense, it will take on a life of its own.

Architects usually can only suggest ideas; they do not have direct manage-ment authority, unlike directors and managers. This forces them to have to sell their architectural approaches.

Life Is Reflexive

Have you ever noticed how your words and actions reflect on you? If you think about this, even a little bit, your actions will be forever changed (see Figure 1-3).

In nearly every circumstance in life, we choose how to respond to those who interact with us. It doesn't really matter what others have said or done; we do, in fact, have the choice whether to respond graciously.

If we choose to be gracious regardless of the outcome, we can feel like we have taken the high road when we leave the situation. In many circum-stances, it is possible to misinterpret other people's intentions with respect to the situation at hand. What may come across as gruff and insensitive comments may actually be related to a poor interaction the person had 30 minutes ago, such that the person is still living in this moment.

One situation in which it is particularly challenging to be gracious is when we are receiving negative feedback about something we have done and care about passionately. On many occasions, the person whose work is being reviewed clearly does not want to receive any negative feedback, and may act as if the criticism is a personal attack rather than an evaulation of the work.

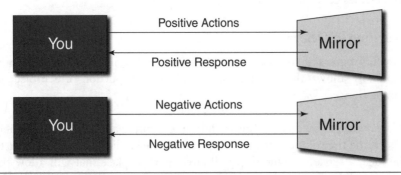

Figure 1-3   Reflexivity is like a mirror: What you say and do is reflected back to you.

Key Point

Working to set up proper expectations for providing feedback and modeling that process yourself can help to build an environment of trust.

Setting proper expectations will encourage the very best ideas to be brought forward, allow suggested course corrections to be stated without offense, and help the work product to be truly improved by having an open conversation about new and innovative alternative approaches.

When going into a review (any review), be mentally prepared to do the following:

- **Listen.** Be prepared to accept the feedback and be willing to change—that is, incorporate the other person's feedback if appropriate, and don't respond until the person has had an opportunity to fully express his or her thoughts. At most, ask for clarifications or paraphrase the statements back to the reviewer to ensure you understand what was said.
- **Don't defend.** It is a natural response, but you will miss valuable information and possibly offend the person who is trying to help (and yes, all reviewers really are trying to help).
- **Be gracious.** You may need to keep this idea at the forefront of your thoughts. Think carefully before you respond and avoid any sarcasm. The edgy comment you may think will be funny (and is likely to get a laugh or two) will not build a good relationship with the person at the other end of the barb. Your careless words may hurt others' feelings and get cemented into their thoughts in a negative way toward you. Ask yourself, "Is this comment really worth it?"

If we respond with anything other than gracious acceptance, we are asking for non-gracious behavior in response.

The best way to prepare for a review is to set the expectations of the meeting in advance based on these bulleted items. Make sure that everyone understands that *all* feedback is appreciated.

Unfortunately, depending on who is in attendance, the negative impressions that are generated from a single meeting can have a long-lasting impact on your career. If you find yourself in a situation where you have not responded graciously, apologize in a humble manner immediately—and mean it. If later on you come to the point where you realize you were offensive in a meeting, go and apologize. It will be hard; you will feel uncomfortable, and your pride may be damaged a bit (don't worry—it will recover).

But, if we don't learn to apologize, we may build up the wall that serves as the barrier against getting promoted in the future. Even worse, we may be laying the groundwork for us to be let go. Relationships are essential to succeed in the world of business—so build them.

Key Point
Part of building relationships is graciously accepting feedback.

The Relationship Between Likability and Competence

In 2005, Tiziana Casciaro from Harvard University and Miguel Sousa Lobo from Duke University performed a study that sought to determine the relationship between likability and competence. Their findings were fascinating: "If someone is strongly disliked, it's almost irrelevant whether or not she is competent; people won't want to work with her anyway. By contrast, if someone is liked, his colleagues will seek out every little bit of competence he has to offer."[1]

From my own experience, people who exhibit caustic behavior in an organization will foster an environment in which open communication is minimized, trust is lowered, and anxiety rises. As a result, the ability to partner with other organizations is greatly reduced, the productivity of the team drops, and quality solutions dwindle. Eventually, caustic individuals are removed from the organization or their ability to influence others is greatly diminished.

Learning to project the behaviors, actions, and words that we want reflected back to us is a critical concept to understand in the journey of moving toward becoming a gracious professional.

---

1. Casciaro, Tiziana; Lobo, Miguel Sousa. (2005). "Fool vs. Jerk: Whom Would You Hire?" *HBS Working Knowledge*. http://hbswk.hbs.edu/item/4916.html

> **Key Point**
> Remember the golden rule: "Do unto others as you would have them do unto you." [Matthew 7:12]

Life or Death for Effective Communications

As you speak, you literally plant words that mean either life or death for your attempt to communicate. They will build up or tear down walls—so choose what you say carefully (see Figure 1-4).

Don't speak negatively about someone. Harsh words will negatively affect your relationship with that person; it is a weed that will take root and grow. Always evaluate the words that you speak. Are they positive or negative? (Choose positive.) Are they geared toward building up or tearing down? (Choose building up.)

In general, you should look for opportunities to build relationships. There are so many ways that ideas, concepts, and information can be represented when you are communicating. Try to pick words that will clearly convey the intent of the message you want to deliver, but do so in the context of the individual you are communicating with.

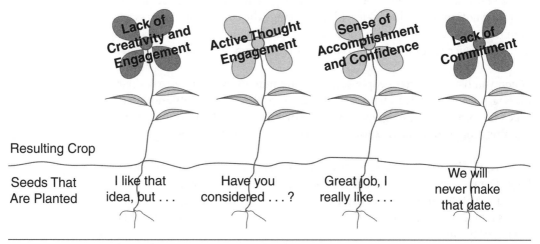

Figure 1-4 What kind of crop do you want? Plant the right kind of seeds.

The message you are delivering should be crafted with the context of the other person or group in mind. If you ever get the chance to follow an executive around for part of a day, you will likely observe that this person has expertly honed communication skills.

Executives and Their Personalized Communication Style

A few years ago, I was walking down the hallway with an executive. On our way, we ran into several people she needed to talk to for a moment. To my amazement, the language she used, the interaction style she chose, and her voice inflections varied from person to person. She made the context switch to be completely focused on the specific individual immediately and framed the conversation to be meaningful to that person.

The interesting thing was that the order of the people in the hallway started with a software developer. As we progressed down the hallway, the employee grade level of the people increased incrementally up to her boss. It was striking to see the fast-paced context switching all happen within a matter of 5 to 10 minutes. It impressed on me the need to focus less on what I had to say and more on communicating the message in a meaningful way to the person I was interacting with.

The ability to dynamically switch context based on who is present is a hallmark of many successful and powerful people, such as Bill Clinton and Margaret Thatcher.

I am someone for whom technology is the center of the universe; I love to think and consider all the aspects of technology and truly immerse myself in it. The notion of "selling"—learning to change the context of the message I am trying to deliver to match the audience I am interacting with—is a distant, faint voice that I have had to consciously work on developing for years.

When you listen to what people say, there are many ways to interpret their messages. Often we have a tendency to hear "negative" statements and interpret what others are saying relative to our own context when, in reality, we are often not even in the mix for the information being presented.

Usually, the best approach is to hear what others have to say in a positive light. Even if you cannot manage that feat, try to ignore or forget the points that appear to be negative (see Figure 1-5). If you receive the negative statements and let them take root, they will affect the way you interact with that person over time.

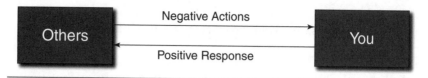

Figure 1-5 Reflect a positive response even when you receive negative messages.

Always choose to respond in a gracious fashion. (Do not respond by trying to get even—it does not work.) If the message is truly offensive, deal with it directly and let the other person know you do not appreciate or wish to be exposed to similar comments or behavior. If the comment or behavior is repeated, you may need to get the individual's superiors involved.

In the role of architect and in life in general, it is critical to maintain and build positive relationships. One of the best ways to accomplish this goal is to speak and hear words that emphasize the positive.

Integrity and Honesty Without Bluntness

In the world of architecture, integrity and trust are vital for success. The challenge is how to present information in a manner that does not offend the other parties involved.

Two distinct challenges arise here:

- Delivering information that has "integrity and honesty" without overwhelming bluntness (see Figure 1-6). Otherwise, due to the blunt-force trauma you inflict, the person you are trying to help may be completely offended and never hear the useful information you were attempting to deliver.

Figure 1-6 Integrity should *not* be used with blunt force.

- Being so cautious about not offending the person that you sugar-coat the message, so much so that the needed information is never delivered.

Let's look at the bluntness aspect in more detail. After the presentation of information, you still want to have a positive relationship with the person. All too often, people end up being unnecessarily offended or put on the defensive simply because of a poor delivery of vital information.

Here are a few key questions to consider when you feel the urge to "be perfectly honest":

- Will the information presented have a meaningful impact on a future event? (If not, why are you bringing up ancient history? It is better to let sleeping dogs lie.)
- Could the information be misinterpreted? (You need to ensure that sufficient context is given.)
- Are you avoiding personalization of the issue? (It could appear that you are attacking the person and not the issue.)
- Will you preserve the valued relationship with the person or group after this conversation? (In the end, relationships are nearly always more important than isolated issues. If this is a reoccurring problem, you may need to be a little more direct.)
- How would you feel if the situation were reversed?
- Is the person or group already aware of the information? Have they already taken corrective action? (Don't pile on to a situation that is already being addressed; instead, find a way to pitch in and help.)

Nearly any time you need to present critical information where corrective action is required, emotions tend to run high and the likelihood of blurting out "raw" information increases. For some people, it is helpful to count to five internally (to let your mouth catch up to your brain) before launching into a diatribe.

Now that the information is being presented in a non-blunt ("friendly") manner, we need to ensure that proper, unbiased information is being delivered. In Minnesota, the phrase "Minnesota nice" is used to describe the pattern of not discussing the real issues in the name of being "nice." The real issues tend to live just below the surface and get discussed everywhere except for the one area that needs it most. Here are a few more questions to consider:

- Are you talking to the right person or group? If not, are you trying to get advice on how to deal with the situation or are you just engaging in gossip?
- Do you have all of the necessary information?
- Is the information that you do have correct?
- Have you heard from all affected parties?
- Are you presenting facts and not conclusions? (The conclusions you draw may have no basis in reality.)
- Is the matter being dealt with in a timely manner? Is this going to matter in a month? Will anyone remember what you are talking about?
- Why are you agreeing to do this task (e.g., just to avoid conflict, to avoid responsibility, you were told to do this)?
- Are you "complaining" about this situation at the coffee line and not at a meeting? Be willing to share your thoughts at the meeting in a gracious manner; complaining to everyone else *after* the meeting does not help. (If the problem is just with one individual, however, a private conversation with that individual may be warranted.)
- When you are asked if everyone is on board at a meeting, do you bring up unresolved issues and concerns you have at the meeting, or do you complain later in a hallway conversation? If you don't bring up your issues, are you willing to forever hold your peace?

In many ways, issues are like weeds that live in a garden. You don't always have to deal with them immediately, but in general you are best off dealing with them quickly.

Don't Bury Issues—They Will Come Back

Are you avoiding dealing with a particular issue because you are afraid of the consequences? Are you afraid of the confrontation? Normally, reality is not as scary as our imagination. It sometimes seems as if many of the issues we face in life are tests. Until we pass the test, we seem to get the opportunity to deal with the issue repeatedly until we can manage it confidently.

Have you ever been in a meeting and been asked if you agree with the proposed direction of a project, when, in the back of your mind, you hear a soft voice saying, "No"—yet you proceed to nod your head in agreement? The meeting concludes, and 5 minutes later you run into a few people from the meeting. They are having a conversation about the "agreed upon" direction and are picking it apart with a variety of scenarios. You chime in with more issues concerning the direction chosen (the same information that triggered your internal voice earlier).

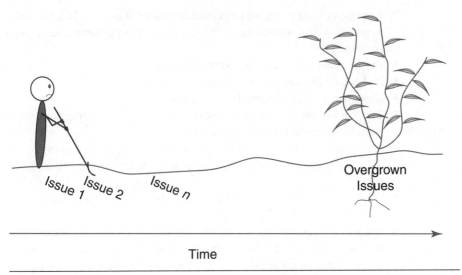

Issue 1   Issue 2   Issue n   Overgrown Issues

Time

Figure 1-7   Buried issues eventually turn into real problems, so deal with them now.

Months pass by, and now the project has some major issues (see Figure 1-7). You recall the hallway conversation where this exact set of issues was discussed. A realization strikes you that this current pain and suffering could have been avoided if anyone from the post-meeting hallway conversation had chosen to speak up.

Sound familiar? It does to me. I have certainly had this experience more than once during my career.

Over time, I have learned to listen to the small voice that says "No." Today, when I am in meetings and we are moving toward consensus, and there is a final roll call for group consensus, if I don't agree, I say, "No," and we work through the issues. Sometimes, it turns out that we are all in agreement, and it is just a few items that need to be clarified. Sometimes it turns out that we don't all agree, but do agree that the direction is the best given the priorities before us.

After the meeting, if I hear others discussing the "issues" surrounding the decision in the meeting, I will bring up the point that everyone needs to hear this information. I then suggest we need to discuss this issue at the next meeting or reconvene the meeting to review the decision.

Deal with the pain upfront: The issue will simply grow and turn into a genuine problem if it is not dealt with. Confronting problematic issues most likely will not be fun, but if they are not addressed now, there will likely be real pain in the future.

Provide a Professional Service

The role of an architect is that of a service provider. You need to provide the best quality of service regardless of how you feel, how others are treating you, or how many different ideas are bouncing around in your head. It is all about others and the service you are trying to provide—it is not about you.

Have you ever noticed that most people in management seem to have worked in the service industry at one time or another?

Have you ever worked in a situation where you needed to interact directly with customers on a regular basis? I have—and I can confirm that such an experience directly affects how you approach interacting with others. Some of my own service experiences include mowing neighbors' yards, being a clerk in a golf pro shop, being a clerk at a drug store, teaching math classes, and waiting on tables. I never realized it at the time, but all of these jobs influenced me, and continue to influence me today, in ways I never imagined.

Think about the last time you walked away from a purchase where you were completely thrilled about the transaction. What was the sales person like? How did he or she act? Now try to repeat those behaviors yourself. Some will work, and some won't—but you should be willing to give them a try.

Let's go over a few of the basics:

- Learn to smile. (Be approachable.)
- Learn proper posture. (Stand up or sit up straight with your feet directly under you, shoulders back, chin up.)
- Learn to engage others in small talk. (Prime the conversation, put others at ease, begin to build a relationship.)
- Learn to focus on others, not yourself. (Be aware of others around you.)
- Be present; be where you are. (The most important place for you to be is where you are at—if not, why are you there?)
- Learn to be helpful. (What are the other person's needs? How can you best help the individual?)

- Learn to be concerned. (The world is not just about you.)
- Learn to be friendly. (Become a friend—the more you interact with others, the higher the likelihood that you will enjoy the work you do.)
- Learn to build trust. (If you say something, do it; if you have an issue with someone, deal directly with that person, rather than discussing the problem with others.)
- Learn to say yes. (Don't find excuses to disengage or avoid what is hard. Are there alternatives that would enable you to say yes?)
- Learn to listen. (Repeat what you have heard; don't draw conclusions; ask questions out of genuine interest.)
- Be knowledgeable; share information, not conclusions.
- Allow choice. (One of the best ways to direct a decision is not to dictate, but rather to present selectable alternatives—it allows the other person to take ownership. The next time you are at a restaurant, watch how your interactions with the waiter or waitress progress.)
- Do not stray from the point at hand and go off on a tangent.
- Be aware of the entire context of the discussion, and do not repeat unnecessary information or stray outside it.
- For the more senior architects, remember that executives are people, too—they have the same hopes, fears, and worries about their communications as you do. Treat them like normal people, and they will respond as such. If the conversation appears to be moving toward blame, try saying, "I don't want to talk out of turn, but is this arguing over blame helping us solve the problem?"

When you approach architecture as a service, you get into the right mindset about what you are trying to accomplish: serving others for the purpose of producing great products that will enable your company to generate revenue.

Forgive Past Offenses

As an architect, you need to be able to work with people regardless of whether you like them or dislike them, and whether they are nice to you or not.

If you have had negative experiences with someone, you need to forgive that person and put the "offense" out of your thinking. If you hang on to an offense from another person, it is like carrying a pebble. Carrying a handful may be manageable, but accumulating a large sack of rocks is not manageable—and it affects you more than the other person.

Consider these things before you choose to be offended:

- In a day or two, if the other person would be unlikely to remember the comment or action that offended you—the person has moved on—you need to do likewise.
- The other person's behavior may be something that is repeated everywhere; it may be just a bad pattern that the individual learned for how to interact with people in general (not just with you). The person may simply be acting out of habit and not consciously trying to be offensive. He or she may have no idea of the impact the behavior has on other people.
- The person may be responding to an event that just happened, and you were "lucky" enough to be the next person the individual interacted with.
- The person's words or ideas may not have been fully baked; perhaps it was a thought in the midst of being formulated that just did not come out right.
- If the person truly meant to be destructive with the words or behavior, you are still better off not receiving the poison—leave it with the aggressor. (If need be, minimize your encounters with the individual until you are able to interact peacefully.)
- Most situations will work themselves out over time, although it may take several years. Eventually, the person will move on or be moved on.
- Sometimes, what you assume to be reality (a certain truth in the universe) turns out to be completely inaccurate. The person you assumed did something did not. The "reason" you thought the person acted in a certain manner was completely a figment of your imagination. The individual may have been acting in a perfectly innocent manner and never intended an offense; the problem arose because of the way you chose to react to a situation with the limited information you had available.

Given that you may have limited contextual information at hand, opt for going with the more positive interpretation of what is happening. In our limited perception, we appear to be the center of the universe. In reality, everyone around you is acting in his or her own context over which you have a limited influence, so the offense you perceive may simply be your own perception.

Choose to travel light when it comes to being offended (see Figure 1-8). This approach will enable you to deal with new opportunities quickly and easily.

Figure 1-8 Choose to leave offenses behind.

Other people truly do not care about the baggage you carry around, so don't carry any. Even if you don't talk about the baggage you carry in regard to a particular individual, it will affect the way you interact with that person in the future. Your body language and eyes will reveal you.

So, just like with a good Web service, choose to be stateless. Respond to just the current input (not the long, long history of what you have likely incorrectly perceived and the other person no longer remembers)—after all, your brain can deal with only a limited number of items (seven—plus or minus two—things) at once. Don't burn your limited bandwidth with out-of-date, useless information. (Be stateless.)

Keep the other person's best interests at heart, and because life is reflective, your best interests will likely be reflected back to you and take care of themselves. Life is odd that way. Most of the things that are truly of value to you take a more indirect route. That is, other people will be nice to you most likely because you have been nice to them. Don't withhold being nice to try to get even—it simply does not work.

Even if the person you are dealing with truly is a complete jerk, you will personally feel better about yourself and be happier having taken the high road. If nothing else, for purely selfish reasons choose to respond positively: It will help you save your sanity and avoid a trip to the local psychologist.

Approach each day like it's a new day with new challenges. Remember the lessons you have learned along the way—not the offenses. You will truly be a happier person.

SUMMARY

The road to gracious behavior begins with the following steps:

- Choosing relationships over correctness
- Learning to delegate
- Realizing that life is reflexive
- Acting as though words have a lasting impact
- Dealing with others with integrity and honesty without bluntness
- Confronting issues in a timely manner
- Providing a professional service
- Forgiving and forgetting past offenses

For technically inclined individuals, working toward becoming a gracious professional not only makes life as a whole more enjoyable, but also opens new opportunities for advancement and growth.

BIBLIOGRAPHY

Briner, Bob. (1996). *The Management Methods of Jesus: Ancient Wisdom for Modern Business.* Thomas Nelson.

Carnegie, Dale. (2009). *How to Win Friends and Influence People.* Simon & Schuster.

Cathy, S. Truett. (1989). *It's Easier to Succeed Than to Fail.* Thomas Nelson.

Covey, Stephen R. (2000). *Principle Centered Leadership.* Simon & Schuster.

Covey, Stephen R. (1989). *The Seven Habits of Highly Effective People: Powerful Lessons in Personal Change.* Simon & Schuster.

Freeman, Criswell. (1997). *The Gardener's Guide to Life: Timeless Lessons Based on the Principles of Gardening.* Walnut Grove Press.

Kilts, James M.; Mandfredi, John F.; Lorber, Robert. (2007). *Doing What Matters: How to Get Results That Make a Difference: The Revolutionary Old-Fashioned Approach* [Audio CD]. Random House Audio.

Maister, David H. (2000). *True Professionalism: The courage to Care About Your People, Your Clients, and Your Career.* Free Press.

Maxwell, John C. (1998). *The Twenty-One Irrefutable Laws of Leadership: Follow Them and People Will Follow.* Thomas Nelson.

Maxwell, John C. (1992). *The Winning Attitude: Your Key to Personal Success.* Thomas Nelson.

Maxwell, John C. (2004). *Winning with People: Discover the People Principles That Work for You Every Time.* Thomas Nelson.

Nightingale, Earl. (1986). *Lead the Field.* Nightingale Conant.

Osteen, Joel. (2004). *Your Best Life Now: Seven Steps to Living at Your Full Potential.* Warner Faith.

Thaler, Linda Kaplan; Koval, Robin. (2006). *The Power of Nice: How to Conquer the Business World with Kindness* [Audio CD]. Crown Business.

Ziglar, Zig. (1994). *Over the Top: Moving from Survival to Stability, from Stability to Success, from Success to Significance.* Thomas Nelson.

Chapter 2

COMMUNICATION

To listen well is as powerful a means of communication and influence as to talk well.

—John Marshall, Chief Justice of the United States

I only wish I could find an institute that teaches people how to listen. Business people need to listen at least as much as they need to talk. Too many people fail to realize that real communication goes in both directions.

—Lee Iacocca, Former CEO[1]

You can have brilliant ideas, but if you can't get them across, your ideas won't get you anywhere.

—Lee Iacocca

In the role of architect, communication is the essential skill and tool that is required to be effective.

Architects typically do not have direct management oversight over the individuals who work on their projects or over others who are more loosely associated with their projects. Their projects typically span multiple departments and potentially multiple business units. As a result of not having direct management oversight, architects' ability to dictate that individuals or groups perform specific actions is limited. The only lever that is really available to them is influence.

For technical staff rising through the ranks of development, the primary focus is on technical expertise. The ability to become a technical expert and communicate that technical knowledge is critical to moving up in the ranks. This skill typically means becoming highly competent at defending your position and surfacing subtle nuances that are potential risks or

---

1. Novak, William. (1987). *Iacocca: An Autobiography.* Bantam Dell.

current problems for a particular project. At this level in the organization's hierarchy, you are asked to prevent problems, find problems, and solve them, all while everyone above you watches your every step. The pressure can be immense at times.

For the technical individual who wants to make that first jump into management (I consider architects to be part of management), the nature of the next rung on the ladder changes dramatically. In particular, the skill set required begins to move toward a wider and more varied amount of communication.

This chapter unveils one of the key essential soft skills needed by an architect: communication (see Figure 2-1).

COMMUNICATION PRINCIPLES

Learning to communicate effectively is a lifelong process—there is always room for improvement. The series of principles shown in Figure 2-2 can help lay the foundation for you to become an effective communicator.

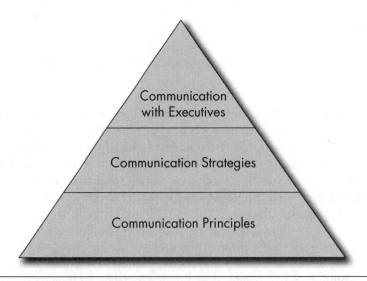

Figure 2-1   Communication for architects is based first on communication principles, second on communication strategies, and third on effective communication with executives.

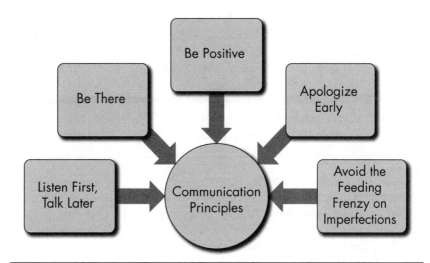

Figure 2-2   Learning communication principles such as listen first, talk later; being there (being both physically and mentally present); being positive; and so on can help build trust with others and make you a more skilled communicator.

Listen First, Talk Later

Have you ever found yourself deeply engrossed in preparing for your next opportunity to speak in a conversation and not really hearing a word the other person is saying? Exactly what message are you sending to the person who is talking to you when you don't listen?

At least on the surface, it appears that you don't care what that individual has to say. Most people tire of this type of conversation quickly when their words are simply ripples through the air with no destination. The person talking may decide he or she has better things to do and work to wrap up the conversation. If you do this only once in a while, the behavior is probably not a big deal. If it is your normal mode of operation, you are building a wall between yourself and others.

Are you listening for opportunities to correct the other person? Do you have a point that you are just waiting to make even though the conversation has moved on?

These things point to us not really listening to what the other person is saying. The person talking cares enough about you to take time out of his or her busy day to give you valuable information. Try to hear it.

When someone is talking to you, look at him while he speaks and try to understand what he is communicating. Give your conversational partner sufficient time to convey his point before you ask clarifying questions. Give him nonverbal feedback, such as nodding your head, to let him know you are paying attention to the conversation.

I believe Epictetus, the Roman slave, said it well: "We have two ears and one mouth so we may listen more and talk the less."

Be There

Wherever you are, be there. There are so many distractions in life (what are you going to do this weekend, how are you going to solve the problem from the meeting just a few minutes ago, how are you going to approach telling your boss some negative news, what time is your kid's soccer game tonight), that it's easy to become lost in minutiae.

Generally, you have the ability to consciously think of only seven plus or minus two items at any given time. If you are filling your head with all of these other, irrelevant thoughts, you will not be where you are at—and if others are talking to you, you may completely miss what they are saying. If they ask you a question, you may need to have them repeat it. In this situation, you are truly wasting other people's time, and they are likely not going to be happy about it. If there is an executive in the room, you are making a lasting, negative impression: What a waste of money.

Read some time management books and get a daily planner in which you can capture all of the items you need to be concerned about. Within the planner, prioritize your tasks (for the day, for the week, and so on) and identify the amount time you plan to devote to each task. This approach will allow your planner to remember everything and free up valuable space in your conscious thinking to focus on what is immediately happening around you.

If you are truly not needed at a meeting, don't go. If you are needed, be there and nowhere else.

I have found that by sitting up straight, putting my feet directly under my seat, taking notes, and actively looking at the person who is speaking, I will naturally be engaged in what is going on in the meeting and project a positive image of active engagement both verbally and nonverbally.

No matter where you are, be there.

Be Positive

When you are presenting information, you always have a wide array of ways to deliver it at your disposal. The information needs to be factual and accurate, but it can be colored in many ways.

You can choose to present information from a positive perspective or a negative perspective. You may be biased to focus on one approach rather than the other based on the outcome you desire. You can also be neutral, however, and just present the facts as they stand with no emotion, although this is often difficult to achieve.

From a communication perspective, it is easy to focus on the negative areas. Typically, these areas are internally generating fear. (When I feel fear approaching, I try to use it as a signal that FocusEd Action is Required.)

As an architect, you need to avoid unnecessarily biasing information and allow others to choose which information to heed. You may provide them with alternatives, but they should stand on equal footing. You need to perceive what is possible, not plant seeds of doubt.

Apologize Early

During the course of your day, you may have stated something inaccurately or done something that was not quite right with respect to another individual. Learn to eat your pride and go apologize to the affected parties. Issuing a heart-felt apology will not be fun or easy, but you will gain the respect of the parties and demonstrate that you are trying to grow and become a better person.

If you apologize, the other party will likely overlook the matter and forgive you for any pain and suffering caused. What may have been an embarrassing matter can be turned into something positive. Your relationship with that person now has the opportunity to grow instead of shrink.

The internal tendency is to want to bury the situation and move on. Unfortunately, you have just buried a seed and are allowing it to grow into a (potentially poisonous) weed that may affect you for a long time. The offended person may choose to hold on to the offense and remember it for a long, long time. The individual may also repeat the story to others to demonstrate the type of person you are. As a result, your ability to interact with the person and potentially others will be diminished. Eventually, you may forget what you did, but the other party may not.

When you do apologize, be clear about what you are apologizing for and mean what you are saying. If you are insincere in issuing an apology, the false note you project will likely make matters worse. If you cannot bring yourself to be sincere, avoid the apology, but your goal should be striving to build positive relationships with the people with whom you interact. Avoiding apologies moves you in the wrong direction and limits your personal growth.

Avoid the Feeding Frenzy on Imperfections

When you are in review meetings (e.g., product concept evaluations, requirements reviews, design reviews, code reviews, test reviews, product launch reviews), there are often times when imperfections surrounding the reviewed item begin to surface. The authors of the item will naturally feel a little uneasiness as these imperfections are revealed.

Out of common courtesy, once three or four issues have been raised in a particular area, don't pile the criticism on higher and deeper. If you have additional items that need to be addressed, write them down so that the affected individual has a log of points to refer to later. These types of feeding frenzies, in which one person becomes the target of everyone's wrath, can significantly impact the remaining portion of the review in terms of its effectiveness.

Here are some valid approaches to a review:

- Ensure that the focus is on the item being reviewed and that the comments are not personalized toward the parties who produced or created the item. In other words, focus on the what or the how, not the who.
  - Avoid words that personalize the comments such as "you" or "your."
  - Find ways to express the goals of why you are requesting a change: Does the change tie into a marketing strategy, a general architectural principle, or a company/department goal?
- Focus on ways that the work item can be improved (not just because a coding guideline is not being followed, but why the change will help later on). The person whose work product is being improved needs to learn not only how to do things better, but also why these improvements will help.

- Find opportunities to say positive things about the work that has been done. Most people feel very defensive and finding positive points will help soften the blows. All participants need to realize that the goal is to produce excellent work and that everyone is being held to the same standard—it is a community effort.
- Make sure that everyone at the meeting is participating; sitting on the sidelines is not an effective use of the company's time.
- Model the behavior you are looking for; demonstrate when your work is being reviewed that it is okay to "bring it on." The goal is to produce excellent work and continually improve. In other words, it's not about you; it's about striving for excellence.
- Be gracious: How would you like someone to approach giving feedback to you if the roles were reversed?

It is important that any issues are documented—not just for your benefit in tracking, but also as a log for other interested parties. If there really are a significant number of items that require attention, a follow-up review may be necessary.

COMMUNICATION STRATEGIES

Moving beyond core principles for communicating, you can employ a series of strategies to demonstrate a consistent and effective communication style.

Prefer Yes over No

Architects are often consulted to determine the feasibility of a project and to provide alternative solutions that vary from strategic to tactical, and are accompanied by various cost options, to enable business partners to make judgment calls on the value of making the investment for a particular project. The role of the architect and the project estimating team is not to determine what is being built, but rather to determine how it will be built.

The answer that we are trying to drive to is "Yes, we can build this, and here is the related information." The information produced needs to include things such as alternative approaches considered, project risks (and possible mitigation strategies), the assumptions being made, and outstanding issues that need to be addressed.

We are not looking for ways to say, "No, this project is not feasible, but we can build this other project (by eliminating all of the hard problems from the hard project we are saying no to and replacing them with features we want to build)."

Key Point

As architects, we need to look for ways to say "yes."

If a project or task isn't feasible, however, we need to state that assessment tactfully immediately, explain why, and offer alternatives. This is often the case when legal, regulatory, or compliance reasons mean that "no" is the right answer. Certainly, other exceptions exist as well: The person making the request routinely looks to pawn off work, the request will violate a company policy, or another priority work item simply does not give you sufficient time to successfully focus on satisfying the request. In these cases, be clear about why you are saying no.

If an executive asks you to do something, you should ascertain the priority of the request. If it is a high-priority request, you should *always* analyze the impact of not doing other tasks and give the feedback to the executive. This will enable the senior manager to have the information needed for making a priority call between tasks. It will also help you avoid a potential sticky situation later—if you have to explain why some other important task has been dropped without another manager's knowledge.

Learning to say yes can take many alternative forms. Generally, it involves finding a way for the person or the project to move forward. It doesn't necessarily mean taking on the task or request yourself; perhaps you can provide a reasonable set of alternatives or direct the person making the request to others who can move the process closer to solving the issue at hand.

For most projects where feasibility information is requested, the most desirable approach is to make a buffet-style set of options available where the costs, risks, strategic impact, and valid combinations are clearly laid out. This strategy puts the requestor in the driver's seat and allows him or her to determine the solution that provides the highest business value.

Providing a set of options to select from will naturally help build good relationships with your customers and coworkers.

Establishing Trust in the Sales Process[2]

Think about the last time you bought a car, built a house, or made a major purchase. The perceived success or failure of the purchase was largely determined by the interactions that you had with the sales person or contractor.

The sales person likely listened closely to what you wanted and put you in the driver's seat for deciding what you wanted by providing the following information:

- Available options
- Costs of the various options
- Benefits of the various options
- Options that go well together
- Risks associated with various options
- Known problems or defects with each option

The sales person likely did not push you in one direction or another, but helped elicit your needs and seek a solution that provided the highest value to you at the lowest cost. To do so, she likely had to lower the priority she assigned to her own self-interest.

By putting your needs first, the sales person helped establish trust. This trust enabled you to feel like you made an informed decision with someone acting as a partner.

When anyone asked you about your new purchase, you likely raved not only about all of the various aspects of the product, but also about this great sales person (and recommended that sales person for anyone else interested in making a similar type of purchase), thereby beginning a *virtuous* sales cycle.

As an architect, you need to be that sales person. You need to be trustworthy.

Reserve Your No's for Special Occasions

From an architecture perspective, there are only so many times when you can simply say no. The majority of the time, you must provide alternatives for how something could be accomplished (along with the costs, risks, and benefits of each approach). The final decisions ultimately lie with the project owner (whoever holds the purse strings).

---

2. http://thenichereport.com/2010/04/establishing-trust-in-the-sales-process/

Figure 2-3 Save your no's for black tie events—that is, use them sparingly.

At other times, a "no" is appropriate (see Figure 2-3). Typically, this rejection needs to be backed up with a rationale of significant depth to counter any necessary questioning. The likely areas of contention will be related to the normal key constraints of any project (performance, cost, time, and scope).

Here are some considerations for saying no or avoiding saying no:

- With respect to deadlines, it is acceptable to say no when the request defies the laws of physics in calling for the execution of all of the steps of a project (e.g., hardware acquisition and provisioning, planning, development, required training, testing, fixing, and deployment) within the deadline given. It is not acceptable to say no just because the job seems hard, you don't quite feel like it, or there are other competing priorities (perhaps the current request is about to become the highest priority—although it may be worthwhile listing this as a risk). State competing priorities neutrally so that an executive call can be made as to relative importance.
- Questions to ask yourself:
    - Am I acting with integrity? Does what I publicly said in a meeting match what I am saying in the hallway? If you truly have issues with the request, you need to bring them up even if it is not to your benefit. As always, this action needs to be taken in a gracious and respectful manner.
    - Which alternatives exist that might eliminate the "laws of physics" issues? Think out of the box. If this were your company, how would you solve the problem? (And no, the answer is not to fire everyone around you.) If you don't have expertise in a particular area, could you bring in contractors who do have that expertise? Has someone else solved a similar problem? Can you bring that person in or at least ask him or her questions? Are there any proofs of concept that could be implemented quickly to lower the risk of the project in certain areas? Do you need more time to properly estimate the project?
    - Are there others with whom you could brainstorm the solution?

- Could you define the project in stages, with deliverables set for each stage (major release)? This phased approach would allow you to potentially seek funding for each stage individually and allow you to address what you know first. Later, as you learn more, you can estimate the next phase and possibly exit the project if it is determined that the next stage is truly not feasible or does not provide sufficient business value to proceed.
- If you don't say no, you may be doomed to a death march—the project that is characterized high visibility, unending hours of toil, and a customer who is never quite happy. Proper expectations-setting is required upfront to avoid this outcome.
- Special circumstances may sometimes influence the decision to say yes or no. For example, during periods when layoffs or outsourcing are prevalent, a more delicate approach may be needed. Everyone is a little more on edge in this kind of climate, and project negotiations become much more challenging.

It is rarely acceptable to simply say no or to simply state just the facts. Be prepared to cohesively explain the rationale for why the decisions that are being made are, in fact, good business decisions. This is best approached by weaving together the facts, the rationale behind the facts, and the interplay of how this rationale supports the desired business goal.

As an architect, you are in sales. You need to be prepared to sell the solution even when questions arise. During the questioning, it may appear that opposition to your position is rising when, in fact, people are actually probing to validate the solution or their understanding of the solution. They ask questions because they likely will need to be able to sell what is being proposed to their part of the organization later.

You need to believe in the solution being proposed. If you don't really believe in what you are selling, your body language and eyes will give you away. Your insincerity is like the scent of blood in the water: You will likely invite a more detailed set of questioning and it may feel like sharks are attacking. In some real sense, you may have brought this interrogation upon yourself by not being prepared. You need to understand things in enough detail that you believe it is, in fact, possible to achieve what is being proposed. You need to have asked and answered the hard questions yourself before you propose a solution to others.

If at all possible, try to avoid actually saying the word "no." Instead, explain the rationale behind the decision given the context of the person or group you are interacting with.

Avoid the Urge to Get Defensive

Often in a conversation, when we hear things that don't put us in a completely positive light, we may make excuses; we may look for ways to deflect the words and blame others, thereby avoiding shouldering any responsibility ourselves; or we may look to clarify the statements by putting a more positive twist on them. Resist the urge to respond. Instead, wait, and take in what is being said.

In all of the responses described in the preceding paragraph, the conversation has shifted away from genuine interest in the other person to being about you. The act of listening has, at a minimum, temporarily ended. We also begin to send up yellow flags to our conversational partner: "Let's steer the conversation in a different direction—one where I am not involved." Consider the body language you are using—crossed arms or a turned-away head says, "I'm not listening."

Ask yourself this question: How can I learn from what this person is saying? Typically, he is giving you information that may not be pleasant for you to hear, but the engagement is still an opportunity for you to take the information and grow personally.

One exception to the rule of avoiding the urge to defend yourself is when the issue at hand involves company policy or your integrity. If statements are being made that you were actively involved in matters that are directly in conflict with your company's policies or that you did not act with integrity (assuming, of course, that you have acted properly), you need to address these statements immediately. You may want to phrase this point as a clarifying question, such as "Are you saying that I did X?" If the other person says yes, be clear in your response that this is not accurate. If the person says no, thank the individual for the clarification.

Hear Suggestions as Collaborative Improvements

Seek first to understand, then to be understood.

—Stephen Covey, Author/Speaker

From a software development perspective, the opportunity to critique or be critiqued seems to occur with great regularity. There are software reviews, design reviews, architectural approach reviews, unit tests, functional tests, defect tracking, simply asking others for help, a one-on-one with your boss—the list goes on and on. In all of these situations, there is the opportunity to personalize what is being said to being about you.

Once you have shifted the conversation to being about you—instead of being about the work products or some incident—your natural defenses are likely to kick in. At this point, your ability to hear anything becomes limited; your natural "fight or flight" response begins taking over, and your brain directs your body to begin pumping adrenaline into your system to prepare you for self-preservation. The valuable information that is being communicated to improve a work product is gone. From a business perspective, it is in everyone's best interest to make a work product as good as it can be, because the more value we are able to add to the product, the better the return on investment the company has an opportunity to make.

If you can avoid personalizing the conversation, your ability to hear what the other person is saying greatly increases. Try to find out what she is really saying (even if you don't agree). Get to the point where you can restate her idea in a manner that captures the essence of what she is trying to convey. Typically, the other person simply wants to be understood. She's not necessarily looking for you to agree with her. As you listen and gain an understanding of the salient points that are being shared, you can build a shared mental model.

Key Point
Clarify understanding by listening and reiterating what has been said.

Learn Others' Communication Needs, Including Your Own

In the world of architecture, you will routinely interact with a broad set of individuals. You may or may not have interacted with everyone in previous meetings. The challenge is to quickly learn what people are saying and how they are saying it to begin "reading" the meeting.

It is essential to watch for key moments where decisions can be made; to recognize issues or concerns that are arising; to reinforce core concepts that can help you focus the direction of the meeting and enable the meeting to be drawn to a successful conclusion. To recognize these key moments, we need take in all of the information—both verbal and nonverbal—that is being given to us.

Watching others' behavior tells us how to best interact with each person. Because every individual is different and has different needs relative to communications, an architect must adapt his or her means of message delivery to those needs to ensure effective communications.

The key point is that we need to adapt our interaction style based on the communication needs of *each* member of the audience. Some people respond visually; this preference can be identified by use of phrases such as "I see your point." Others need to listen and take in verbal detail; they can be identified by use of phrases such as "I hear you." Still other people are emotionally and tactile in their interactions, as can be identified by use of phrases such as "I feel concern about . . .".

In addition, most individuals' body language (e.g., slouching, sitting attentively, crossing the arms, interacting with others, or using hands while talking) gives you volumes of informational cues about where that person is at with respect to the current meeting or gathering. In fact, a major challenge with conference calls is that you are not able to see the body language of the others on the calls. As a consequence, you don't get the same amount of feedback to help direct the conversation. In turn, it is easier to overlook some of the subtleties of issues, concerns, or ideas that should be addressed or explored. If you listen carefully, you will still be able to hear variances in participants' voice inflections, the tone of their voice, the speed of their delivery—all of these aspects help to give feedback about the effectiveness of the communication.

Another challenge with conference calls is that you may not know everyone on the call and may not have an internal profile or context about common patterns of how the person likes to relate to others. To help overcome this lack of knowledge, at the beginning of the meeting, do the following:

- Gather the name of each person on the call.
- Make a point of acknowledging each person.
- Note all participants' interaction style, approach to the call (i.e., attitude, word, tone of voice), and role.
- Use this knowledge to guide interaction in future calls.

Online presentations, such as WebEx, are better than conference calls in that at least you are able to see what others are currently reacting to. These visualizations also help to direct the conversation.

Videoconferencing, in which everyone in the meeting has a live video feed of themselves, can be a significant improvement over just a conference call or online presentation. Our ability to interact with the majority of other participants is likely to significantly improve when we are able to have live visual feedback or a picture of the person, because it makes the interaction more personable.

One key aspect of this type of interaction to keep in mind is that not only are others telling you in multiple ways what they think of the current interactions, but you are also giving them similar information (see Figure 2-4). You need to consciously be aware of the messages that you are physically conveying to others in a meeting.

Keep these items in mind during the meeting:

- Are you smiling?
- Are you sitting up attentively?
- Are you nodding in agreement?
- Are you giving eye contact to those who are speaking?
- What kinds of voice inflections or tone of voice are you using?
- Are you dressed in a similar fashion to others in the meeting?
- Are you truly listening to understand?
- Are you taking notes?
- Are you being confrontational?

All these items make up a package that lets others know or confirm the consistency of the message that you are delivering. Are you telling a sad story and smiling? If so, that kind of inconsistency takes away from the integrity of the information that you are attempting to deliver.

Work toward developing a complete personal communication package in which what you say and how you say it both deliver the same message; this consistent presentation will improve your ability to communicate effectively.

Figure 2-4 Your body language speaks loudly—so be careful about what you are saying.

Think on Your Feet

Be prepared for questions to be asked at any time. There will likely be no advance notice when questions are posed; that is, you will not have any time to prepare a well-reasoned answer. The questions can come from nearly any direction (those above you, those next to you, and those below you within the organization).

As an architect, you need to be comfortable with immediate context switching—that is, taking everything that is currently bouncing around in your head, pushing it onto the stack of things you need to remember, and dealing squarely with what is in front of you in a contextual manner with your full attention. This practice is better known as "thinking on your feet."

When this happens, try these patterns for dealing with the situation:

1. Focus on who is asking the question. What is that person's context? What information might the individual need to know to understand your response? Is it appropriate for you to respond to the question being asked?
2. Think of a three-point explanation and, if possible, include a supporting business rationale. In your limited time, try to build a cohesive picture of what your answer is trying to communicate.
3. If the request is for a decision to be made, pause and think about the organizational impacts of what you are about to say. As this decision is propagated through the organization, how will other groups respond?
   - If you have placated the person who asked for the decision and other groups will clearly take the brunt of the impact, you should recognize that a whole series of unpleasant conversations will be scheduled with you for the near future.
   - You may want to consider making a decision that leaves every group involved slightly unhappy. Typically, if you can accomplish this feat, you are probably on the right track with respect to negotiating. When everyone has some skin in the game, all parties are much more likely to be cooperative in the future. If nothing else, they realize they have not been singled out and can now focus on solving the real problem at hand.
   - Interestingly, at this point (where everyone is slightly unhappy), everyone becomes more reasonable and more real alternatives may turn up that make the solution simpler, faster, and cheaper. Be prepared to say yes to this answer when it shows up—it is likely the truly innovative solution.

- If your answer will have a negative impact, show how others are also "suffering." As the cliché goes, misery loves company—the joy of shared unhappiness may make swallowing the pill a little more palatable.
- Of course, a decision that leaves every stakeholder happy is sometimes possible and is always preferable.

COMMUNICATING WITH EXECUTIVES

Executives are a unique breed of individuals in any company. Their responsibilities are broad. Their communication, leadership, and relationship skills are well honed. Learning to communicate with executives takes time and practice, but you only get a chance to lock in the first-time impression once—so be prepared.

Executives Thrive on Trust, Loyalty, and Consistency

Executives have an unquenchable thirst for trust, loyalty, and consistency (see Figure 2-5).

When you are interacting with executives (especially the ones who have oversight of the areas you work in), you need to focus on establishing and building both trust and loyalty. As you continue to work with them, the information you present needs to be consistent: You can't tell senior managers one story one day and a totally different story the next day. Avoid biasing the information you are presenting to make yourself look good or to make

Figure 2-5   Executives have a heightened need for trust, loyalty, and consistency. Deliver these.

others look bad. Concentrate on the facts in as succinct and direct way as possible, recognizing that executives are busy people.

When you are meeting with executives, do not roast other individuals who are not in the room. Such behavior demonstrates that you are neither trustworthy nor loyal.

When you are presenting information, provide facts, not opinions about people. Facts are something that can be dealt with rationally, even by the person who is not in the room (assuming you have properly distributed the information—the person who is not in the room should not be blindsided when the executive asks that individual about the facts that you gave).

I have been in meetings where the executive called the other person being discussed into the room and verified all of the information I gave. Be sure that the story you are telling is one you want to repeat in front of the other person, because you may get the opportunity to do so immediately.

Prefer Clarity over Completeness

As a general rule of thumb, the amount of detailed information needed is inversely proportional to the person's level in the organization. In other words, developers will want and need a tremendous amount of information to build something, whereas an executive will need only high-level summary-type information about a project during a regular status update. That information needs to be clear and concise, however. You need to give executives the right information and provide the appropriate context, consisting of more business information and less technical information.

Executives are likely to not care about all of the technical information. They will want to know that you are well versed technically, but they don't have time to consume all of the project minutiae. One of the primary reasons that such sifting occurs is because executives must operate on a basis of trust due to simple time constraints. They are looking to delegate the responsibility for ownership, execution, and oversight to you. They want you to deal with the issues, planning, and other aspects of a project.

What executives do want to know is this:

- Which risks exist that may cause the project to not be delivered on time and on budget? Are these risks being managed?

- Which strategic assets are being created that can be leveraged for current or future projects?
- Who are the "rising stars" within the organization?

Executives demand that you give them accurate information. They expect you to be consistent. Once you give an answer, you need to stick with it—so choose your answers carefully.

Some executives may choose to dive deeper into a particular facet of a project. This area of exploration is likely the area you are least prepared to speak to; the executive may be probing to find out where the boundaries of your knowledge and oversight are.

During a meeting, if you get to a spot where you don't know or are unsure of the information, be clear that you do not know, but state that you will follow up with the information that was asked for. And always do follow up: If you don't, you are putting your hard-earned trust at risk.

Your best course of action with executives is to put your cards on the table—that is, let them see everything (the good, the bad, and the ugly). You may have an unsettled feeling about being completely open and vulnerable, but such behavior increases your standing in the areas that executives prize most—trust and loyalty.

When the time comes that you truly do need executives to get involved, you will have established a critical relationship that will allow you to partner with these senior managers.

What executives do not want to know is the disputes that may be occurring on the project. The fact that department A has a conflict with department B is really *your* problem (and you need to deal with it). If you ask an executive to get involved with "solving" a dispute, you and the parties involved are likely going to be very unhappy with the outcome. Executives seem to have a sixth sense of what the most painful resolution to a dispute is and choose it. For this reason, you are well advised to be succinct and stick to the relevant facts explained at a level suited to the needs of the executive rather than an IT person.

Don't Surprise Executives

When it comes to escalating issues, executives don't like surprises, especially the kind where they need to act in a very short span of time, the number of remaining options is small, and the likely outcome is that they will need to communicate a bad message to the rest of the organization (see Figure 2-6).

Most project risks brew slowly: They are known by those parties who are on or near a project. If you listen carefully, you will hear the information floating all around. Unfortunately, the buzz about these risks may not always rise to those who need to hear it.

People naturally try to put their best foot forward when interacting with senior members of management and executives. As a result, they have a low desire to present something that may not be seen in a positive light

Intermediate-level managers will not appreciate a risk being exposed to their boss or their boss's boss without having an opportunity to craft their message—that is, the sales pitch around the risk. The risks need to be exposed early, given that they tend to increase in size over time. It is often a judgment call as to when to inform others about trouble brewing; there is no magic to knowing when the right time is. As a general rule of thumb, you are far better off having exposed the risk early rather than forcing senior management and executives to deal with the cleanup efforts when it's too late to fix the problem.

If you find that your boss or member of management is not communicating needed information to the executives, you may need to deliver the information yourself. (If you decide to take this course of action, be extremely cautious in doing so; there may be other factors at work that you may be unaware of.) When you do deliver your message, make sure that all intermediary levels of management are aware of the risk. They need to have been given the opportunity to formulate a plan of action for dealing with it. Again, it's all about trust and loyalty.

When executives know about a risk early on, they are much more likely to be able to successfully help manage it and minimize the negative impacts

Figure 2-6   Executives don't like surprises. If you have bad news, deliver it early.

surrounding it. If the executives are surprised, they are not going to be happy. If you haven't destroyed their trust in you (which you worked so hard to establish), you may be on the road to doing so. You may also be minimizing the amount of support you will receive later from the unhappy executives when promotion opportunities arise.

SUMMARY

The road to becoming a great communicator begins with these steps:

- Communication principles:
    - Listen first, talk later.
    - Be there.
    - Be positive.
    - Apologize early.
    - Avoid the feeding frenzy.
- Communication strategies:
    - Prefer yes over no.
    - Reserve your no's for special occasions.
    - Avoid the urge to get defensive.
    - Hear suggestions as collaborative improvements.
    - Learn others' interaction styles, including your own.
    - Be prepared to think on your feet.
- Communicating with executives:
    - Executives thrive on trust, loyalty, and consistency.
    - Prefer clarity over completeness.
    - Avoid surprising executives.

For technically inclined individuals like myself, working toward becoming a great communicator is challenging. I have a tendency to want to analyze and thoroughly think about all the different facets of a problem—at times, literally closing out the outside world. The rewards for focusing on becoming a more skilled communicator not only make my vocational life more enjoyable and geared toward career advancement, but also make my personal life more enjoyable.

BIBLIOGRAPHY

Bick, Julie. (1997). *All I Really Need to Know in Business I Learned at Microsoft*. Simon & Schuster.

Burnett, Mark. (2005). *Jump In! Even if You Don't Know How to Swim*. Ballantine Books.

Carnegie, Dale. (2009). *How to Develop Self-Confidence and Influence People by Public Speaking.* Simon & Schuster.

Decker, Bert. (1996). *The Art of Communicating: Achieving Interpersonal Impact in Business.* Crisp Publications.

Frank, Milo O. (1986). *How to Get Your Point Across in 30 Seconds or Less.* Simon & Schuster.

Kawasaki, Guy (2008). *Reality Check: The Irrelevant Guide to Outsmarting, Outmanaging, and Outmarketing Your Competition.* Portfolio.

Mason, John. (2003). *The Impossible Is Possible: Doing What Others Say Can't Be Done.* Bethany House Publishers.

Maxwell, John C. (1997). *Becoming a Person of Influence: How to Positively Impact the Lives of Others.* Thomas Nelson.

Murphy, Kevin J. (1992). *Effective Listening: How to Profit by Tuning into the Ideas and Suggestions of Others.* Eli Press.

Rothman, Johanna; Derby, Esther. (2005). *Behind Closed Doors: Secrets of Great Management.* Pragmatic Bookshelf.

Wetherbe, James C.; Wetherbe, M. Bond. (1993). *So, What's Your Point.* Mead Publishing.

Woodall, Marian K. (1996). *Thinking on Your Feet: How to Communicate Under Pressure.* Professional Business Communications.

Chapter 3

NEGOTIATION

In business, you don't get what you deserve, you get what you negotiate.

—Chester L. Karrass, Business Negotiation Trainer

My father said: "You must never try to make all the money that's in a deal. Let the other fellow make some money too, because if you have a reputation for always making all the money, you won't have many deals."

—J. Paul Getty, American Industrialist

During a negotiation, it would be wise not to take anything personally. If you leave personalities out of it, you will be able to see opportunities more objectively.

—Brian Koslow

For architects, negotiation skills are critical first to get a project moving toward success and later to keep it running smoothly.

When you first become an architect, you are likely to encounter a few days when you walk away at the end of a day and wonder what just happened. How could (what appeared to be) a minor decision manage to take on a life of its own and have (what appears to be) the entire organization turned upside down, so that now your boss is not the least bit happy with you?

Slowly, as you replay the sequence of events, you begin to realize that the root cause of the issue is not technical in nature, but rather social in nature—the sworn enemy territory of all technical people.

You begin to realize that the organizational alignment to support the decision was simply not in place; the decision had not been pre-socialized to account for all of the many factors (likely nontechnical) that were at play. Now you and your boss must face the unpleasant experience of undoing the organizational disaster that has unfolded.

A wide variety of architectural roles may be embodied within an organization, from enterprise architects to platform architects to application architects to research architects. The responsibilities and areas that require negotiation for each architect role vary, but one thing is certain: The ability to negotiate is a key asset for all architects.

This chapter focuses on negotiation as an essential soft skill for architects.

NEGOTIATION PRINCIPLES

Whenever you engage in the process of negotiation, you always want to adhere to the series of principles shown in Figure 3-1. These are your guideposts for negotiating fairly to all involved parties, including yourself.

No Surprises

When you are negotiating, you need to operate in such a manner that no one will be surprised at the outcome of the decision. Afterward, effectively communicating the decision to all affected parties is important to maintain the structural integrity of the decision. Otherwise, reasons will be invented for why a decision was made, rather than facts being the basis of the ensuing conversation. Be cognizant of the fact that rumor and innuendo can be dangerous things when it comes to morale, relationships, and delivery of a project.

Figure 3-1   Core negotiation principles

If you don't disclose pertinent information when you are negotiating with your would-be partners, they will not trust you in the future and likely will not be willing to compromise on critical factors that may be needed to ensure a project's success. To avoid this problem, be open and honest and present the technical facts.

If your boss does not know that an important matter is being negotiated, engage him or her quickly to find out if other aspects of the decision need to be contemplated. Just as when you are hiking up a mountain, those above you likely have information or experiences that you simply are not aware of yet. A full view of the context, including nonfunctional requirements and all of the stakeholders, is essential, but is often the purview of management rather than the architect.

Don't Waver on Decisions

Let your yes be "yes" and your no be "no."

When you make a decision, stick with it. Constantly changing project decisions are an organizational nightmare. People leave a meeting understanding what has been decided and begin making other decisions based on that understanding. They begin resource planning and shift departmental priorities to accommodate the direction that was agreed upon.

If you come to realize that a decision was truly a poor one, make the necessary adjustments and change your decision (but take this approach sparingly). If you do change your decision, you should let the affected parties know what has changed and which adjustments they need to make or consider. Sticking with a poor decision could be detrimental to the overall project. The important idea is to try to minimize the changes in project direction.

One way to help solidify, document, and communicate decisions is to maintain an architectural decision log (more on this later).

Delegate Authority, Not Accountability

Typically, I try to find a handful of key individuals within each group that I need to work with and with whom I can establish a high-trust relationship. I work toward giving these individuals opportunities to grow in their negotiation and decision-making capabilities. This delegation can help both me and the organization in the following ways:

- It builds rapport and shared collaborative success.
- It has long-term implications in building the capabilities and careers of those persons who accept the responsibility.
- It lessens my workload.
- It increases my overall effectiveness.

One of the essential things to realize is that you are not delegating accountability. In fact, to ensure the success of the people who accept these responsibilities, you need to give them a sense of where the boundaries of the delegated authority are.

Key Point

Regardless of the outcome of the decisions of those who have operated with your delegated authority, you are still accountable for the outcome.

When decisions have the potential to make a major impact, your delegates should recognize the need to consult with you or directly involve you in the decision-making process. In all cases, the decision and its rationale need to be communicated to you. This will enable you to be consistent in what you say to others to help reinforce the decision that was made. Otherwise, you may undermine both the authority you are attempting to delegate and the trust of the person you are trying to build up.

Seek Help When You Are in over Your Head

Sometimes, you may be in a situation where you simply do not possess the authority, the skills, or the background knowledge to make the decision that is being requested of you. In these scenarios, you need to be clear with others that this is not a decision you can make. You need to quickly bring in superiors who do have the authority to make the decision, or who can get you access to the help you need to inform them which decision should be made.

If the negotiation is completed and you later realize that you did not have the authority to make the decision, you need to quickly communicate the situation to the person or group that does have the authority. Communicate all the information you know and the rationale behind your decision. By quickly sharing this information with the person or group that does have the authority, you ensure that they have a chance to step in and take some remedial action, if necessary. Of course, they may also decide to let the decision stand.

Key Point
"Open" and "honest" should be the bywords in all architectural decisions.

By being open about what happened and ensuring the real decision-making authority that your mistake will not happen again, you can build trust with the affected parties, even in the face of a potentially bad situation. Don't repeat this behavior; you will destroy trust if you do.

Don't Cover Things Up

If you make a decision that ends up going bad, take some remedial steps:

- Take responsibility.
- Apologize to the affected parties at the earliest opportunity.
- Let others know what happened.
- Let others know why it happened.
- Don't try to transfer responsibility to others by blaming them.
- Don't go silent when others are trying to figure out what is going on.

If people know that you are honorable in your decision making, they will gain respect for you and will want to work with you in the future.

Praise the good work done by others who help you remediate the situation. Doing so will make them more likely to help you in the future.

Be nice to people as you go up in an organization, and they will be nice to you.

If you go down, remember that all organizations change their personnel and hierarchies from time to time.

Do the Right Thing Even When It's Hard

If you say you will do something and have committed to doing it, you need to deliver on your promise no matter what:

- Whether it was in public or in private
- Whether it was verbal or written down

Doing the right thing may cost you personally in terms of time, money, and effort, but it will be a great lesson learned. Your partners will see that you say yes or no only when you are fully committed to a negotiated decision.

NEGOTIATION STRATEGIES

Whenever you are engaging in the negotiation process, you can use a variety of strategies to help you achieve a successful outcome. The strategies discussed here are intended to improve your negotiation skills.

Listen to Your Gut Feelings

If you have some underlying reservation about a decision that is about to be made, you need to get it out on the table during the decision-making process. It may be extremely uncomfortable to deal with the conflict or the perceived personal risk, but you need to learn to express your gut feelings on matters. You lose all rights to say, "I told you so," when you are at the decision-making table. In fact, it not really a good idea to say, "I told you so," even during side conversations.

This gut feeling should nudge you to do some investigations to help validate or invalidate your thoughts on a particular point. In the near future, you will likely be required to deliver some real facts to back up a gut reaction, even if your qualms are not completely formulated. If necessary, say "I believe this needs further thought, so I will get back to you," and then give a date when you will have completed your investigation.

It is also important not to be "the boy who cried wolf" or you will start to be ignored very rapidly. Have at least some measure of facts and metrics behind your gut feelings before expressing them too broadly.

Manage to Yes

During the course of the day as an architect, you are constantly bombarded with tough decisions that need a quick response. Typically, the real decision is figuring out how to remove an obstacle from a group or individual to allow that group or individual to move forward. The obstacle can take many forms:

- Tool selection
- A modeling problem

- An obstinate person in the group who is fixated on "his" solution versus collaborating
- An executive who needs critical status information
- Two groups that cannot agree on who needs to do something

Essentially, obstacles are either (1) social and organizational or (2) technical. The technical obstacles are usually the easier ones to overcome.

In situations characterized by social and organizational obstacles, your goal is usually to get the other person to say, "Yes, I understand and have what I need, so I can now move forward." Typically, to accomplish this goal, you need to listen carefully to the request and look for the real question that usually lies just beneath the surface. Watch for the body language cues that signal whether something is being concealed or whether a point is of particular concern.

Don't try to solve the problem immediately. Try to keep the other person talking as much as possible to get as much context as possible. If necessary, gather an impromptu meeting of others who can give an even broader context for the issue. During the conversation, repeat the information that is being conveyed to ensure that you understand what is actually being said.

Once you feel that you can accurately restate the problem and truly understand where the other person is coming from, you can transition from hearing and understanding to finding a solution. At this point, it is important to write down a summary of your understanding that can be shared and confirmed.

Has the person who is asking for a decision had the opportunity to think through the problem on his or her own for a while? If individuals haven't learned to do critical thinking on their own, you are doing them no favors by simply giving them an answer. Replaying the problem context summary to them can help them firm up their own thoughts.

You may want to consider having the person who is making the request go back for a while to think through the problem and then return to you with three approaches and a recommendation. If you don't do so, you are simply enabling yourself to be a crutch for that person, and your coworker is missing a potentially valuable learning opportunity. Of course, to avoid a negative project impact, you may need to seed ideas after a time.

Once you believe that the person is in a position to articulate alternatives and a recommendation, you can provide additional alternatives, thoughts, and rationale for why one recommendation may be preferred over another. In this way, you can develop a broader context of points to consider in decision making—a valuable lesson in itself.

Once that person is at the point where she is willing to say "yes" to the decision, she should be saying so not because you are in a position of authority and you said so, but because she understands and is able to personally defend, own, and drive forward with implementing the decision.

Don't Find the Differences

In the technical realms, being able to find the nuances and subtle variations to a problem, to a technology, or to a design is an essential skill for being considered competent and allows for flexibility in dealing with different requirements. When it comes to making technical decisions, working through these minor variances is what allows great software to be produced.

When it comes to making higher-level decisions (softer negotiated decisions), the need for finding differences begins to diminish. The goal becomes one of finding a viable solution. This solution may not always be technically "the best," but rather something that is technically "good enough" and serves many other needs and aspects of the project. As mentioned previously, cost, time scales, and quality are always in balance. To satisfy any two of these demands, the third has to be flexible, and potentially some sacrifices may have to be made in that dimension.

Find the Common Ground

> *Former adversaries can come together to find common ground in a way that benefits all their people, to let go of the past and embrace the future, to forgive and to reconcile.*
>
> —Bill Clinton, U.S. President

When different organizations come together to solve a particular problem, they come to the table with their own preconceived notions of what is best, what is easiest for them to do, what their areas of expertise are, which patterns are valid and invalid for framing problems, and so on.

As the various groups come together, the first issue to be addressed should be finding a common goal (see Figure 3-2). A common goal is one that everyone can agree upon (in other words, what the requirements are). Next,

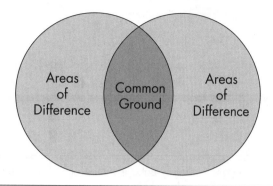

Figure 3-2 Look for areas of common ground, not differences.

the groups need to define success. That is, how will they determine that the problem is satisfactorily complete? Finally, they can begin working through and determining how to solve the problem.

To successfully accomplish these tasks, everyone at the table needs to put their biases aside and look toward solving the problem in a way that truly meets the success criteria without biasing it toward one group's preferences. If one group demands to have everything their way, both groups should take the time to explore the issues at hand:

- Find out what the root causes of their positions are (in private, if needed).
- Find out what their top priorities are. (You may be able to get them to give on less important points.)
- Find out if they are in a position to make a decision. (If not, you may need to bring the real decision makers to the table.)

Successfully resolving differences means giving ground and making sacrifices. It is best approached by trying to "step into the other person's shoes" and to "see their point of view" when addressing the problem. When the opposing views and needs are understood, finding common ground is much easier.

If General Agreement is Not Possible, Make Everyone Slightly Unhappy

Our first aim is that everyone should be happy with an approach, but we must recognize that such an outcome often isn't possible. Balance is needed. An odd fact of life: To make a diverse group work effectively together,

Figure 3-3   If everyone is slightly unhappy, then all parties are more likely to work together cohesively.

sometimes everyone in the group needs to be slightly unhappy (see Figure 3-3). This slight unhappiness occurs because all parties have to put one or more of their biases on the table and give up something. This compromise allows members of another group to successfully complete their tasks at a reasonable cost.

In the end, decision making is an ecosystem that requires all members to bond together for the common good, and to put personal preferences aside. The outcome of this give-and-take is that all parties believe that they have taken the higher road and, consequently, they feel good about the decision. Obviously, if everyone agrees on an approach upfront with no dissenters, then it is a win-win situation.

In situations where not everyone is in broad agreement when others are informed of the decision, the fact that every group had to give a little makes the broader organization more likely to accept the decision. Conversely, when one group is continually favored over others, resentment builds in the organization and may lead to unnecessary roadblocks in the future.

Use Negotiation as a Means of Improvement

The negotiation process can dramatically improve an idea or a solution, assuming everyone puts their best ideas on the table. This situation is a bit like polishing a rock: The forces at play remove the rough edges and will likely deliver a smooth result.

Effective negotiation may also allow ideas or projects to get killed early on, before significant resources have been expended. This is truly adding value to a company.

Negative return on investment (ROI) can be a very bad thing, as it forces other projects to make up for the shortfalls in what may have been a bad idea. Early identification of projects doomed to failure is a good thing—even if it is not fun, and even if it was your pet project that got eliminated.

There is a fine balance between letting creative ideas flourish and killing them early on without proper investigation. This balance is achieved through collaboration.

NEGOTIATION PREP WORK

Before you begin negotiating for anything, you should obtain the critical background information on the decision. This information can be vital to your ability to successfully negotiate an outcome that is well received by all parties involved.

Know What Is Negotiable

There are three categories of negotiability:

- Areas that are non-negotiable because of integrity reasons, such as morals, company rules, and integrity of solution. You absolutely cannot give on them.
- Areas that simply have no meaningful impact. You can give on them.
- Areas that may have a significant (but not lethal) impact on the outcome of the negotiation. Typically, there are pros and cons surrounding cost, performance, functionality, resources, or aesthetics that need to be accounted for with such decisions. This category is the most important area on which to focus your attention.

As an architect, you are constantly shifting focal points for negotiation. Because architectural responsibilities are broad, you are often in a position where decisions are made and not all affected parties are present for a particular decision. You need to be prepared and capable of representing the best interests of all those who are not present. You need to understand their positions and their likely desires with respect to the discussion at hand. If the decision will likely have a significant impact or if you do not have the requisite skills to properly represent them, you may want to request that the decision be postponed until the most impacted "owners" can be present.

If the decision cannot be postponed, arbitrate with their interests and potentially multiple groups' interests balanced in your arbitration. You will want to ensure that that no group is disadvantaged to satisfy the other parties that are involved.

Play fair.

Don't play favorites—including when it comes to your favorite pet technologies. If you are biased and you know it, make sure that valid reasons—such as cost, timing, functionality, or strategic reasons—are driving the decision.

Be prepared to explain the rationale behind the decision to those who were not present. Knowing common rules of thumb employed in the organization, standing business principles, and strategic company directions can help you craft an explanation that enables everyone to recognize that they were treated fairly and that you are trustworthy. Ultimately, you need to describe the rationale in terms of balancing cost, time, and quality, including why certain tradeoffs were made. If the decision making is fair, balanced, complete, and fact based, you will likely win over a dissenter.

Be able to show all parties where they won and where they lost—don't let someone else surprise them with these outcomes if you were not clear about what was at stake in the decision that was being made. Clarifying gains and losses will not always be fun, but dealing with hard conversations in a direct manner will increase your credibility and build your relationship with the team members involved in the negotiation. In turn, the team members will be able to act rationally when others come to them and ask the tough questions about why a particular decision was made.

Later, if appropriate (the decisions that have been made may not be for public consumption), let others know why a particular decision was made. If you don't let them know the real reasons, people will try to fill in the blanks, and you may end up unintentionally feeding the rumor mill.

General architecture best practice is to use an architectural decisions document to document every decision, its background, the alternatives, and the reasons why the choice is the right one. This kind of log will also help future projects justify their adoption of your choices or demonstrate the rationale for why change is needed.

Know How to Surf the Organization

Within an organization, there are often two separate structures: the published hierarchical reporting structure that people operate within, and the unpublished hierarchy of decision makers within the organization. The latter group forms the ecosystem for how decisions are really made. This group or individual is the "mover and shaker" behind nearly every important decision and often influences the strategy that determines where the organization is heading.

Learning who the real decision makers are within an organization is critical for your success (see Figure 3-4). If you convince them of the technical and/or business merits of a particular architecture and obtain their buy-in for a particular decision, the rest of the organization will naturally follow. The hallway conversations and other corporate communication channels will likely validate the direction with this individual or group whether you explicitly include them in the decision-making process or not.

Even if you are unable to acquire this individual's or group's buy-in for the proposed direction, such decision makers can help you to understand the obstacles you will likely face if you truly wish to pursue your intended direction.

Establishing trust with this group or individual is critical. You will need these decision makers to act as a sounding board for your decisions and the rationale behind your decisions. They will likely have a broad understanding of the following questions:

- What impact will your decisions have?
- Who needs to be included for a successful implementation of your desired direction?
- Which alternatives should you have considered, and why were those alternatives not considered acceptable?

Surfin' the Organization

Figure 3-4   Learn how to surf the organization. Know how and where decisions are really made.

Be aware that when you are lower in the organization, talking to the "oracles of truth" may be considered a breach of commonly accepted practices when it spans organizational boundaries.

For an architect, organizational boundaries need to disappear. You need to be able to talk to whoever has the information you need to successfully package a decision or solution, thereby ensuring it has the best possible opportunity for success in the marketplace. (Note that I did not say technology, technical success, or personal success—the goal here is to sell the product or otherwise improve the company's business prospects.)

Architecture is about the business. It focuses on representing, communicating, and building on the key points of a technology or even a nontechnology solution that has beneficial impact to the business in some way.

Seek a Collaborative Context for Key Decisions

When a major decision is approaching, one of the best things you can do is to individually meet with all of the stakeholders in advance to establish a collaborative context. During each encounter, take note of the person's body language and words. These will highlight what is important to the individual—and special attention should be paid when the words and the body language contradict each other. This information will help you to learn and understand the context in which the stakeholders are operating. It will also allow you to understand which areas are non-negotiable from their perspective.

One of the most important reasons to take this step before a formal, group-wide meeting is to allow each person the opportunity to work through his or her thoughts in a nonconfrontational environment. If you are springing information on team members at the meeting to which they have had no prior exposure, you may get them to start from a defensive position and may be about to enter into a long, painful boxing match where everyone takes their corners and comes out swinging. If this situation begins to unfold and emotions start to rise, your hope for a reasonable solution is gone. Such friction may result in you getting to meet with the first common executive between the two groups and going through an arbitration process that is likely to make all groups unhappy and set the project on a long and painful path.

The obvious solution to this dilemma is to prepare for the meeting by constructing a neutral agenda that provides context to avoid surprises. This agenda should highlight the key points of concern and importance for the architecture; after all, abstracting key components of a solution is what architecture is all about.

If you can understand upfront where all team members are coming from and understand their priorities, your odds as an architect to package a solution that everyone can buy into increase dramatically.

Ideally, if you have been able to reach a consensus prior to the meeting, the negotiation should become more of a report out and everyone will be happy. In such a case, everyone has had an opportunity to socialize possible outcomes prior to the meeting, and most likely all severe challenges to the possible outcomes will have been addressed.

When you begin with collaborative decisions at the beginning of a project, team members are likely to embrace the same collaborative spirit as the project moves forward.

Your success as an architect often lies in your ability to informally collaborate with decisions and to avoid a public arbitration where people's perceived egos are on the line and where winners and losers are publicly displayed.

Such informal collaboration is best done on a face-to-face basis or minimally via a phone call. Avoid email for these types of interactions.

Learn the Culture

Often when you come into or interact with a new organization, you may think that you have all of the answers. A typical thought may be, "What could they have been thinking when they organized their systems this way?" This type of pompous attitude will not serve you well as an architect. Nevertheless, you can learn by targeting the "gaps" that make you feel this way and documenting the differences. The "why" can be very telling about what the real drivers in the hierarchy are and who has real power.

There are a variety of ways to solve problems, and many of them will likely serve the business well. Your job is twofold:

- Quickly learn the nuances of the new area
- Make decisions from within their context

Regardless of the organization's appearance, its employees are usually making the best decisions they can for the business, driven by ordinary self-preservation/self-interest.

You need to learn the company's language, preferences, and common beliefs. In a real sense, each organization is a tribe or a number of tribes. You need to respect its way of doing things and find a way to become an honorary tribe member for a given context. Often business units are tribes as well as enterprises in their own right. The project will dictate whether the needs of the whole organization "tribe" or those of the business unit "tribe" take precedence, and how you ultimately balance the priorities.

As an architect, you need to establish trust and work toward building relationships. This focus will enable you to work effectively with other team members and make both your job and their jobs more enjoyable experiences. Once you establish trust, uphold that trust even when you are with other tribes; don't make fun of certain idiosyncrasies they may have or betray their trust in other ways. Choose to be honorable.

Let Others Understand Your Thinking

Because you cannot be everywhere at once, and because architects are typically massively overbooked from a commitment perspective, you need to work toward ensuring that others are prepared to act and make decisions that align with your perspective. To accomplish this feat, you should work with others to mentor, train, and explain the principles, rules of thumb, and company strategies that you use to make your decisions.

> **Key Point**
> Take the time to document key principles and standards, and the reasoning behind them.

Such sharing of knowledge allows others to represent your wishes without constantly requiring your presence. It also helps the broader organization to become more efficient and better aligned as time progresses.

NEGOTIATION WRAP-UP

When you finish negotiating, the process of moving beyond the outcome can be as important as the actual negotiation itself. Several key aspects need to be managed afterward.

Ongoing Defense of the Decision

When you make decisions, be prepared to address questions that come from above you, from below you, from peers, and from interested outside parties. Invariably, not all possible scenarios or factors may have been taken into account. As a result, you should follow these guidelines:

- Be prepared to listen to what your critics are saying,
- Limit your likely strong desire to explain or defend yourself.
- Say "thank you." (They are trying to help in their own way.)

You need to commit the rationale of the decision to long-term memory. You are likely to be quizzed on the rationale for some time into the distant future—most likely at the time you are least prepared for it.

One characteristic of a good architect is being able to recall detailed information accurately at a moment's notice (sometimes months or years later).

Maintaining an Architecture Decision Log

It is amazing how often people forget the outcome of a well-negotiated decision after several months have passed. The issue may then be raised again and begin to be relitigated, and the short version of history repeats itself. Taking the time to maintain a decision log can help keep the project focused, and avoid unnecessary diversions. The architectural decision log should include the following details:

- State the problem
- State the decision itself
- State the rationale of the decision
- Identify other options considered
- Explain why the other options were rejected
- Identify the details of when the decision was made
- Identify who was involved in making the decision
- Be publically available to all team members and stakeholders

Sometimes new circumstances do arise that justify a reevaluation of a decision. This impetus may come from customer usability studies, from sales and marketing, from new tools or components, or from competitive market conditions.

If the change in direction is nonsubstantive, there is no real problem: You can likely make the change and simply move forward. If the decision significantly affects cost, performance, functionality, resources, or aesthetics, however, all stakeholders should be involved in deciding the outcome.

If possible, one person should be the final decision maker. If the variance will have more than a 10% to 20% impact on cost or possibly cause the project to miss key milestones, you will likely want to create a change request (CR) and be more formal about the decision and the rationale behind it. This process helps ensure that stakeholders are kept abreast of subtle changes and their likely impacts, and it provides a documentation trail later on if one is needed.

Sometimes You Win, Sometimes You Lose

When the dust settles and a project is well on its way, you will discover new information that will be an indicator of how you fared in the negotiation process. There are three likely outcomes:

- You won, and you have some positive margin to deal with the normal set of hiccups. This will be an enjoyable ride.
- There is no real margin. Things are tight, but can be managed; you just need to suck it up.
- You lose. You will likely have to hurt other areas to recover from this blow; in the worst case, the loss may not be recoverable without a significant business decision to apply additional investment.

No matter how hard you try to negotiate in good faith, at some point you will have to deal with all three of these scenarios. Facing down these prospects typically gives veteran architects their many battle scars. Of course, it also allows them to make wise decisions in the future, because they have had the opportunity to make a bad decision, survived the ensuing battle, and now know which pitfalls to avoid.

"We learn by doing" means we don't hold back, but rather get on with the task at hand and learn from the outcome. That resilience, in turn, is where the adage "We learn from our mistakes" comes from.

Sometimes, when faced with a win-lose decision the best thing to do is make it win-win by changing the rules, changing the players, or changing the game.

Learning from Delegating

It is okay for some delegated decisions to go wrong. This kind of mis-step is an opportunity for you and the other individual to learn how to be more effective in communicating the boundaries of decision making, your intended direction for decisions, and the many other aspects that go into communicating decisions.

The fact that things may not go as planned is a routine part of life. Embrace mistakes, apologize for them, and then learn from them.

Take the responsibility and think through how things could have gone differently. Avoid the temptation to relegate the individual away from any future decision-making involvement.

Take the time to talk to the person. It may not be fun, but if you keep the person's best interest at heart, he or she will respect you for having an open and honest conversation about what happened and how to best approach this type of matter in the future.

If the person does a great job, let the individual know that, and freely share this information with others—especially those people above the individual in a direct reporting chain. Such feedback helps the person's managers, directors, and vice presidents understand who has potential within the organization.

If your delegated decisions routinely go wrong, you need to seriously evaluate what is happening. In such a case, others are not likely to be at fault; instead, the person in the mirror is the probable culprit. Reflect on the process you followed in delegating and the way in which you communicated the boundaries and principles, and learn how to improve it for the next time.

If you are unable to adequately delegate authority, you need to take some additional steps:

- Look at reducing your workload, so that you can be near decisions.
- Look at taking some training classes.
- Look for someone who can mentor you in the skill of delegation.

SUMMARY

The road to becoming a great negotiator begins with the following concepts:

- Negotiation principles:
  - Avoid organizational surprises.
  - Don't waver on decisions.
  - Delegate authority, not accountability.
  - Seek help when you are in over your head.
  - Don't cover things up.
  - Do the right thing even when it is hard.
- Negotiation strategies:
  - Listen to your gut.
  - Manage to yes.
  - Don't find the differences.
  - Focus on finding common ground.
  - If general agreement is not possible, make everyone slightly unhappy.
  - Use negotiation as a means of improvement.
- Negotiation prep work:
  - Know what is negotiable.
  - Know how to surf the organization.
  - Seek a collaborative context for key decisions.
  - Learn the culture of those involved in the decision.
  - Let others understand your thinking.
- Negotiation wrap-up:
  - Be prepared to provide an ongoing defense of the decision.
  - Maintain an architecture decision log.
  - Realize that sometimes you win and sometimes you lose.
  - Learn from delegating.

Learning how to negotiate is a challenging skill for anyone. For the technically inclined, it is a taller mountain to climb.

Although all soft skills can be learned, it takes an internal commitment to set in motion your personal growth in the area of soft skills. For me, a concerted effort geared toward reading, training, and mentoring has gotten me farther down the road. It is an ongoing effort to constantly be focused on how I can improve and to learn from the mistakes I make.

Consider taking time to study human behavioral areas such as body language and psychology, as understanding these areas can to help refine your negotiation skills.

BIBLIOGRAPHY

Carnegie, Dale. (2009). *How to Win Friends and Influence People.* Simon & Schuster.

Faber, Barry. (2001). *The 12 Clichés of Selling (and Why They Work).* Workman Publishing.

Lencioni, Patrick. (2005). *Overcoming the Five Dysfunctions of a Team: A Field Guide for Leaders, Managers and Facilitators.* Jossey-Bass.

Maxwell, John C. (1997). *Becoming a Person of Influence: How to Positively Impact the Lives of Others.* Thomas Nelson.

O'Connor, Joseph; Seymour, John. (2003). *Introducing NLP Neuro-Linguistic Programming.* Thorsons.

Patterson, Kerry; Grenny, Joseph; McMillan, Ron; Switzler, Al. (2002). *Crucial Conversations: Tools for Talking When Stakes Are High.* McGraw-Hill.

Rothman, Johanna; Derby, Esther. (2005). *Behind Closed Doors: Secrets of Great Management.* Pragmatic Bookshelf.

Torre, Joe. (1999). *Joe Torre's Ground Rules for Winners: 12 Keys to Managing Team Players, Tough Bosses, Setbacks and Successes.* Hyperion.

Chapter 4

LEADERSHIP

Management is doing things right; leadership is doing the right things.

—Peter F. Drucker, Father of Modern Management

Leadership is the art of getting someone else to do something you want done because he wants to do it.

—Dwight D. Eisenhower, U.S. President

The supreme quality for leadership is unquestionably integrity. Without it, no real success is possible, no matter whether it is on a section gang, a football field, in an army, or in an office.

—Dwight D. Eisenhower

You don't lead by hitting people over the head; that's assault, not leadership.

—Dwight D. Eisenhower

The role of an architect is, by its very nature, founded upon the concept of leadership.

Have you ever been on a project, not as a manager, and just wanted someone to do something? On the surface, it seems like a minor request, but the person has a completely different idea and his or her answer is "no." In your mind, you begin thinking, "What's your problem? I asked you nicely . . . just do it." As you rephrase the request, your frustration level starts to rise, the other person's frustration level starts to rise, and yet there is no visible momentum toward your goal being accomplished.

You begin to tire and realize that it may have been a shorter path for you to just do the job yourself. Unfortunately, you don't have the time, and you really need this person to complete the task. So, you reluctantly ease off and begin to listen. Internally, you begin to ask, "What is this person trying to say? Why is this individual being so stubborn?"

As the conversation progresses, more light is shed on the situation and the request you initially put forth is changing. The insights the other person provides about what needs to be done are extremely perceptive and your request is improving. The other person is becoming more engaged and now appears to be willing to take on the task.

The task that is about to be done is now far better than anything you could have imagined solely by yourself, and the other person is fully engaged.

This seems like a long road. You have expended far more energy than you could have imagined, but the results in direction seem stunning.

You begin to wonder just who was really the stubborn party. Could it have been you?

This chapter unveils another critical soft skill needed by software architects: leadership through influence without required compliance.

LEADERSHIP PRINCIPLES

Leadership is founded on holding and executing certain principles—namely, the notions of trust, vision, safety, and clarity (see Figure 4-1).

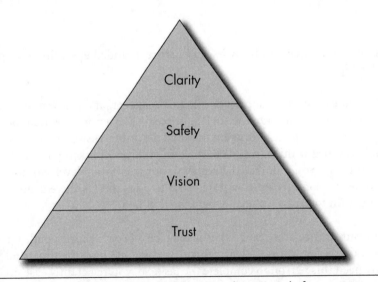

Figure 4-1   Leadership requires delivering on the pyramid of trust, vision, safety, and clarity.

Establish Trust

Leadership is a learned skill. Some people have a natural tendency to lead, whereas for others it is a struggle. Leadership is all about trust.

Trust is in the examples we set for others and the integrity embodied in our actions (I do what I say, and I say what I do). Trust can be established in any number of ways: being an expert in a particular area; successfully delivering a project or part of a project; forming a social relationship; standing up for someone when that individual is in a defenseless position; enabling the other person to succeed; or truly listening to what someone is saying. Once you establish trust, your ability to influence and begin leading others goes up dramatically.

Conversely, if you destroy trust by invalidating the foundation upon which trust was established, your ability to lead others will be dramatically reduced. It will also be much harder to reestablish trust in the future.

If you have proven yourself trustworthy in the past, most people will give you a few breaks if you unintentionally do things that would normally erode trust. They realize that everyone is human and makes mistakes—but their forbearance is a very limited commodity, and you shouldn't rely on it. Instead, learn to apologize and make it more than right.

Establish a Common Vision

Leadership is about establishing a vision that has the right context for each individual. In many ways, it is about sales—about helping people understand what the value of the vision is to them and allowing them to decide if this is where they want to go. The key is to get the right information to each person, because what works for one individual may not work for the next. Organizationally, the same is true. For this reason, you must get to know how each person involved in the project works and understand that individual's point of view and concerns for the project.

Leadership is about establishing a common understanding of the vision. Even though you may have managed to get each person individually on board with the perceived vision, if the understanding of the vision is not cohesive across the team, the organization will not be aligned and relations across teams and other groups will likely be contentious. At best, such discord will cause an unintentional waste in organizational efficiency; at worst, it may cause the project to fail.

As an architect, you should consider using the 4+1 View Model of Architecture by Philippe Krutchen as a means of capturing essential details of the common vision. This approach uses logical, development, process, and physical views of a system, with use cases acting as the "glue" between them and illustrating the architecture for the "plus one." Each view is a facet of a consistent whole. Variations on this model are also possible, but the essence of the approach is recognizing that different stakeholders have different needs, backgrounds, requirements, and even skills to bring to the solution and that, in turn, the architecture needs different views to accommodate each of them. Abstracting the key points of a solution for a particular model of a solution is the main skill underpinning architecture.

Establish Strategic Partnerships (Bring Safety Through Relationships)

Your success as an architect is often determined by your ability to establish strategic partnerships. The need for these partnerships will vary, as different facets of a product vision need to be taken into account.

The business vision for a product is usually established by marketing or new product development. Although you may be able to influence the product vision as an architect, you are usually not the product vision owner.

As an architect, you need to fully understand the business vision for a product, and you are ultimately responsible for turning it into a technical reality. To achieve this goal, you must be able to communicate the vision in such a way that the project team can understand it and lead toward it. By partnering closely with the business and with key members of a project, the architect can help maintain a common view of the vision throughout the product.

When establishing strategic relationships, it is important to focus on those parties who will influence your ability to progress from vision to final project delivery. The individuals or groups who meet this criterion will vary as a project evolves. To succeed at managing these relationships, you must understand the process that your organization follows for projects and product delivery. If you don't, you will engage the wrong people at the wrong time.

For example, you may get to a certain point in the project when what seems technically possible may not be organizationally possible because of the opposition of a person or group that holds the keys to a particular door.

Perhaps your project needs specific hardware to be successful, but due to costs, competitive reasons, or operational standards, you may not be able to get it—and now your project is dead in the water. If you manage these types of dependencies closely and engage the right parts of the organization early on, you can avoid having these potential risks turn into real problems.

As an architect, you also need to establish strategic partnerships with those persons who can act as trusted advisors. These are people whom you can talk to and bounce different ideas off of—who act as a sounding board for your vision. Their input will help you formulate in your mind the organizational approach you may need to take to ensure the vitality of the vision. You need to know how to surf the organization so you can draw upon the knowledge and expertise of a wide range of individuals. An additional dimension arises when you are working with external regulatory bodies, white labeling partners, or third-party delivery partners. In such a case, the "organization" might be a virtual entity crossing company boundaries, but the same requirement for trusted advisors applies.

The more success you have, the more organizational trust you will establish. This factor will, in turn, enable you to have more strategic relationships and the freedom to control more aspects of a project. In the end, you will have more discretion to move outside of what was previously the accepted norm and take the risks that may be necessary for a project to succeed.

Eat Your Own Dog Food (Bring Safety to What You Say)

On any given project, you expect the members of a team to follow certain principles. For example, if you expect the team to act in a transparent way toward you, you need to act in a transparent way toward them, as well as to both your superiors and their superiors. In this environment, team members will find that things you say are things that are safe to do. Follow these guidelines to bring safety to what you say:

- Be transparent.
- Be who you say you are.
- Be open and honest.
- Act with integrity.

Doing these things allows you to establish trust with individuals from various areas of the organization. It also enables to you obtain the information you need to help the project correct itself when it goes off course.

If your coworkers see that your walk and talk don't match, they are likely going to have a lower level of trust in what you say. Later, when you need transparency to understand what is really happening, they may choose to be a little coy about what is taking place.

You need to eat your own dog food; you may discover that what you are asking others to do is not as easy as it first appeared. If you are not willing to do what you are asking other people to do, don't ask.

The best architects have some skills in all of the areas that their architecture covers, so sometimes the "eating your own dog food" criterion can be technical in nature. By following this approach, you see the problem from the other side. This willingness to bend also engenders trust as you will be viewed as "one of us" by the team in question.

Perceive Risk, Assess Impact, and Act (Bring Clarity to Risk)

As an architect, you constantly face situations that demand your attention. Some come to your doorstep (direct requests for intervention), some are simply observations of different project areas that appear to be struggling (lack of movement), and some involve project areas that are moving fast but in the wrong direction.

The key to dealing with all of the commotion and determining where your time is best spent is to do one thing: Determine which risks apply if you don't get involved (not just risks to this project, but also risks to the overall portfolio of projects for which you have responsibility).

Risk Perception

One question I routinely ask myself is, "Will any of the vice presidents get upset if this issue is not dealt with?" If the answer is no, I have more freedom in determining how to deal with the situation. If the answer is yes, I usually have to drop whatever I am doing, jump on the grenade now, and avoid as much collateral damage as possible. In all cases, it is important to take the time to weigh the impact of dropping the other priority tasks to address the "hot potato." One thing to keep in mind is that the vice presidents do have priorities, and all architects need to be aligned to them, even in a crisis.

After things have settled down and have begun to be resolved, you need to ask yourself the following questions:

- How could this situation have been avoided?
- Was some kind of training missing?
- Was bad information disseminated?
- Did some information fail to reach the parties that needed it?

Finding the root causes of these types of issues will help you better prepare for the next project (or maybe just the next week). Learn as much as you can from mistakes and failures. Don't let negative history repeat itself.

When things go off track, take the time to find ways to point this part of the project back toward the vision of what you are trying to accomplish. Find nonthreatening ways to explain what happened and let everyone involved know what things could be done differently.

Be prepared to answer questions from others about what happened. Don't assign blame to people. Deal with the facts in an appropriate manner. Deal with private issues privately.

Deal with Risk Appropriately: What Is a Firecracker Versus an Atomic Bomb? (Bring Clarity to Impact)

When you are assessing the risk of what is happening in a particular project, there is always a balance between stepping in and keeping your distance (allowing project teams to truly own areas of the project).

If the impact is small to moderate, the project team may be best off struggling for a bit and learning the problem-solving skills needed to recover on their own. This is more of the firecracker size impact: The situation will get your attention, but it is manageable.

If the impact of the risk is significant—for example, if the project will fail or be dramatically impacted—you need to step in and help out in whatever way will best resolve the issue. This kind of situation is more akin to an atomic bomb.

Assessing risk tends to be a fairly subtle endeavor. There are rarely red flashing lights to tell you that you have a major emergency on your hands. The effects on the project are usually multiple steps away from the initial root cause.

Part of good leadership is learning to listen to your gut. If someone tells you something and the information gives you an uneasy feeling, you probably want to listen carefully and look into matters in more detail. After you have had time to gather the necessary facts, you can determine the best course of action.

LEADERSHIP STRATEGIES

Leadership strategies provide approaches that can be used to reinforce the principles you are trying to demonstrate. The following strategies will help solidify trust, vision, safety, and clarity.

Use Occam's Razor

"Occam's razor is a logical principle attributed to the mediaeval philosopher William of Occam (or Ockham). The principle states that one should not make more assumptions than the minimum needed. . . . In any given model, Occam's razor helps us to 'shave off' those concepts, variables or constructs that are not really needed."[1]

Being aware of Occam's Razor will enable you as a leader to know how to blend concepts efficiently and effectively. As a leader, you will hear an unrelenting series of suggestions for how to improve, change, or expand the vision. Taking all of this information in and judiciously adding to the concept that is being developed requires an ability to hear what is said, extract aspects of it, and reformulate the argument such that it has intellectual integrity with the whole. The key is to add depth while maintaining clarity and simplicity.

When choosing which changes to include in the scope of the vision, look at the impact on cost, quality, and time scales. Take on board only those changes or refinements to the depth of the project that improve on one or more of these aspects without adversely affecting the remaining dimensions.

Present Visualizations of Information

For most contexts and people, the best way to convey information generally is to put it into pictures. That doesn't mean that the detail isn't written down elsewhere in words; rather, it means that when it comes to abstract concepts, vision, and other elements, a picture gives the necessary context and framework on which to build.

---

1. Heylighen F. (1995). Occam's Razor. In: *Principia Cybernetica* (http://pcp.vub.ac.be/OCCAMRAX.html).

Architectural Visualization

Typically, when I am trying to present an architectural vision, I focus on diagrams that convey key concepts, models, data flow, process flows, assumptions, and risks. Consider using Philippe Kruchten's 4+1 Model View of Architecture as a basis for the information presented. In my own work, I try to whittle my presentation down to 10 slides containing a series of pictures and diagrams that I can address verbally. The idea is to include the key points of the vision and leave out unnecessary details—in other words, to communicate an abstraction, which is what architecture is all about.

Depending on the audience, you will want to vary the conversation to focus on their particular areas of concern. In my own work, if possible, I try to meet with smaller groups. In all cases, I work toward leaving the conversation open to different directions to make sure all of their questions are answered.

If possible, I try to co-present with the business owners. This joint action allows us to bring forward a well-thought-out and cohesive vision of where we want to go.

Generally, when it comes to what is being presented, less is more. Don't put so many things on the screen that the only way to decipher the graphic is to be right next to the screen. Try to break things up so that no more than five to nine ideas are conveyed at a time.

Lead by Keeping Things Focused

Leaders need to know how to stay on point. There will always be a cloud of distractions that surface during the course of a project. Discriminating those distractions that truly require action from those that can be ignored is critical for you to be able to maintain forward momentum. Consider the following questions:

- Will the distraction affect the delivery date?
- Will it affect the cost of the project?
- Will it affect one of the core tenets of the vision?
- Can it be dealt with later?
- Does it need to be dealt with at all?

Focus on staying on point: Drive in a direction that allows you to continue toward your desired end point without introducing new obstacles that will need to be managed later. At the same time, although you need to be focused, you also need to be conscientious of the needs of those around you who are raising issues and concerns that you may be choosing not to address at the current time.

Sometimes, to keep things focused, you need to redirect attention toward other areas of a project that require attention. This diversion may allow some of the nonessential items to wither and possibly drift away.

Leaders need to know when, where, and how to stand up and fight (lead the charge). Occasionally, some areas or items may require you to stand up and hold your ground—that is, they may be areas where compromise is simply not an option. Perhaps the scalability of the solution is being compromised, the cost of what is proposed will simply blow the budget out of the water, or an essential element of the vision is under attack. These types of battles need to be carefully chosen and not waged based on an emotional attachment or reaction to the issue at hand.

Leaders need to deliver a consistent message. Although many clarifications are typically needed to establish a vision, the message that gets delivered needs to have the consistency of a drumbeat. Know what that message is and repeat it. You may potentially say it in many different ways, but you must always deliver it with the same essence.

Sell Based on Context

As a leader, you are selling a concept, a vision, or a goal. When you are selling and working toward getting others to buy into a direction, you need to provide information that is relevant to each person's context.

For example, if you are dealing with an operations team, you need to address the following issues:

- The operational costs
- The potential operational improvements
- The operational risks

This team needs to have the information that allows team members to figure out how this project fits into the organization and what needs to be considered in terms of the organizational vision, mandates, and directives. Remember that introducing new technologies requires improving the skills of the staff and the systems management as part of operationalizing the new technologies, so make sure your project has planned for and arranged for these items and their associated costs.

By comparison, if you are dealing with the software development team, they will want answers to the following questions:

- Which technologies are involved?
- Is training required?
- What are the resource requirements from a hardware perspective?
- What are the resource requirements from a software skills perspective?

Generally speaking, you are showing team members what's in it for them. They may tangentially care about other areas, but their primary focus will be on themselves. Give them the information that is needed for them to be able to build a conceptual model in their heads:

- What is the vision?
- How they can contribute toward realization of that vision?
- What will the benefits be?
- What are the risks they may face?
- How they can help build the future?

Team members need to have enough information that they can go back to their constituent part of the organization and sell what is being proposed.

Following the Crowd (Looking for Opportunities to Leverage)

During the course of any project, there are a limited number of battles that you will want to wage, thereby spending some of your organization goodwill to achieve a particular goal. Your bank account for goodwill is limited, and you certainly do not want to overdraw it—so choose your battles wisely.

As a leader, ask yourself the following questions:

- Has this issue or a similar one been resolved by the organization in the past? If so, you may want to choose a similar resolution if the results are perceived to have been positive. Keep an eye on the differences, however, as neglecting them and the impact they have can make the problem considerably worse.
- Has this technology been used or evaluated within the organization? If no other key factors are involved and the technology was already selected, you may want to consider using it. The operational considerations of bringing in a new technology can be relatively high and are typically not insignificant in terms of training, staff exposure

to its use and best practices, job coverage while team members are attending training sessions, test systems on which to make mistakes and learn from them, consultancy, and other factors. If the benefits are not dramatic, it is unlikely to be worth it to adopt a new technology that will bring only minor improvements given the localized cost, performance, or functional improvements.

Focus Executives on Vision, Not Conflict Resolution

One of the best ways to engage executives is to seek their input from a strategic direction perspective. Their insights—into where the organization is heading, what other organizations are doing, and what their specific future plans are—can help you craft and shape your own vision.

For architects, executives are likely the most important of all stakeholders. It is a good idea to occasionally stand back and "step into their shoes" to see how the vision fits into their perspective given the other priorities and projects. By doing so, it becomes possible to align the vision with the strategies. This approach will also help you determine which of the competing delivery dimensions (cost, quality, and time) can be sacrificed to improve the others.

If the business wants to be first to market, then time is the key dimension. In this scenario, recognizing the essence of time and suggesting quicker, albeit possibly costlier, ways of delivery may be popular with executives and improve the vision further. Remember that technology is part of the business, however, and as such needs to align with business strategies.

By working with executives, you can gain critical allies in helping sell the vision. Part of good leadership is building cohesive organizational alignment.

LEADERSHIP TIMING

A key aspect of being successful in a leadership role is to understand the importance of timing. If the right strategies are employed at the wrong time, what would have normally been smooth sailing can quickly turn into a disaster. The following items will help you develop a context for timing.

Capitalize on Organizational Momentum

When different projects or parts of the organization have had success with particular architectural stacks, software vendors, contracting vendors, or sales channels, you will want to leverage these areas if they can offer something reasonably close to the solution you need. These successes and best practices will usually form the basis of enterprise architecture and standards anyway, so the reuse is likely to help avoid friction with the parties that manage them for the organization.

A significant amount of organizational energy is expended anytime something new is introduced. If your requirements are truly unique and there is no room for adjustment, you may want to consider carving new trails, but only when the rewards for this energy will be significant; be aware of the political dynamics that surrounded the previous decisions. It is usually best to move forward cautiously with these type of decisions. In doing so, engage with the enterprise architects and standards enforcers to get their buy-in and avoid problems later on.

If you cannot find a path that is already being or has been successfully pursued, you may want to look at the larger industry in which your organization operates or in adjacent industries to determine the architectural approaches that have been taken for addressing a particular problem.

As you narrow your choices, keep in mind that most technologies are supported by best practices documents, books, forums, and user groups. In addition, consultancy is usually a means to quickly bridge any skills gap if its cost can be accommodated.

Learn When to Rescue

If you learn that a project you are responsible for is about to start sounding the fire sirens, drop what you are doing, take time to triage the project, and begin formulating the message that is about to be delivered (see Figure 4-2).

Figure 4-2   Rescue a project when the potential harm outweighs the learning opportunity.

If you can step in and quickly avert the issues with minimal impacts, do so (a rescue here is a good thing).

If you cannot easily bring the situation under control, you need to quickly assess the following questions:

- What are the likely impacts of what is about to occur?
- Which alternatives are available for avoiding these impacts?
- What is the best approach?
- How do I go about getting help for the project?
- Who has skills in the problem area?
- Who needs to be brought up to speed? (Transparency is critical.)

Gather and present the facts neutrally and honestly to make sure there is no loss of trust. Later, you can do some root-cause analysis so you can avoid this kind of fun in the future.

Allow Others to Learn

Sometimes, stepping in and solving the problem at hand is not the right thing to do. If the project impacts are manageable, the best option may be to simply allow the team to work though its problems and figure out how to get out of the hole they just dug—experience is always a good teacher.

Although allowing them to continue running into brick walls may not be popular with everyone on the team, the process allows them to grow and learn how to be more self-sufficient. If they have struggled for a while and they are still encountering problems, stepping in to help them overcome some of the hurdles is a good idea.

In my own life, I have learned the most from experience. Denying project team members the opportunity to get the same benefit does no one any favors, even though it may be the expedient thing to do.

Know When to Stand Alone

Sometimes leadership requires the visionary to stand alone. This situation typically arises when new business directions are being pursued, new requirements (at least, new to the organization) are being introduced, or a reengineering effort is being contemplated. These types of efforts normally necessitate that organizations take a fresh look at how to solve a problem.

At these times, the organization is usually more accepting of expanding or altering its technology base.

If you are simply doing more of something that has been done before, you may want to consider ways of increasing the efficiency of how it being done. In contrast, introducing change just because it's a cool new technology or approach is rarely warranted.

Psychologists have outlined a dimension called *options and procedures* that should be considered here. An extreme-procedures person always tries to do what he or she has done before, sometimes even by forcing the use of the wrong tool for a job. As the old saying goes, "To a man with only a hammer, everything looks like a nail. " An extreme-options person always looks for a new approach, just in case it is better than what worked successfully in the past.

In current software development, there is a tendency for options personality traits to dominate, whereas in older support staff, procedures traits dominate. In a good architect, these two extremes are balanced such that the architect chooses a new technology or approach only when it offers a clear and proven benefit—not just because it is cool (see Figure 4-3).

If you truly feel that what is being done is "wrong" and should be approached differently, be prepared to justify the investment required, and be able to show the revenue growth or cost savings that will follow from the investment to correct what is "wrong." Apply caution when dealing with these scenarios, however: Just because something is more architecturally pure doesn't make it better if it has no functional or business value.

Figure 4-3   Choose carefully when to stand alone.

Allow those who are making the decisions of where limited investment dollars should be allocated to make an informed decision. They will be able to compare and contrast your request with other opportunities. Generally, building a better mouse trap is not warranted, although making incremental improvements may be. In addition, there are times when taking calculated risks is a worthy endeavor.

> **Key Point**
> Choose carefully when to stand alone.

Ask for Forgiveness or Ask for Permission

When it comes to leadership, key decision points will often force you to determine whether you want to ask for forgiveness later for the decision you are about to make or ask for permission and risk the possibility that the answer will be no.

If you choose to take the "ask for forgiveness" approach, you need to be fully aware of the risks you are taking on and the likelihood of success. You need to ensure that you will have enough rope so that you will land on your feet versus hanging.

In these cases, the organizational psyche may not support approving the initial effort, but when it perceives a successful implementation of it, the organization will be fully aligned with the new approach. You will also be putting people on notice that you are a calculated risk taker. The key word is "calculated." Make sure you know what you are getting into, prepare mitigation efforts for problems, and develop a backout plan. Also, remember that corporate standards are often the result of a wider strategy or regulation—and bear that point in mind before taking a stand against them.

The downside of this strategy is that you may be putting your boss in an untenable position of explaining why your rogue decision was made and why it failed. This will not be a fun conversation. Your action will have eroded trust, and your scope of authority is likely to be reduced in the future.

If you choose to take the "ask for permission" approach, your boss may assume that you are trying to shift responsibility for a hard decision to someone else. It may appear that you are laying the groundwork for the blame game. You are also setting a precedent for future decision making.

In either case, the route you take will likely not be neatly laid out for you. You will need to follow your own internal compass to find a path you are comfortable with.

LEADING OTHERS

One of the key concepts underlying leadership is "others"—that is, the existence of followers. Your ability to effectively engage others in your leadership hinges on your followers' successful contributions to the goal being pursued.

Allow Others to Contribute (Don't Mandate)

A vision by its very nature is partially cloudy; it is more of a direction than a concrete fixed item. In some sense, a vision is the travel destination. From where you are today, many routes can be taken to arrive at a particular destination. Determining how to get there offers an opportunity to begin engaging others in crafting the travel plans. For an architect, a key task is to identify which parts of the plan are essential and not subject to negotiation. A leader is not a cult leader who is trying to indoctrinate others, but rather is more of tour guide on a shared journey.

To help you identify those areas in which you can be flexible with respect to the vision and allow others to contribute, you need to learn where it is acceptable to be flexible and where rigidity is required. Consider the following questions:

- Which key qualities of the vision cannot be compromised?
- What are the assumptions you have already established? Are they really necessary?
- Are these assumptions documented? (People don't like surprises.)
- Do you believe in the vision? If you don't believe in where you are going, why should others?
- Are there other ways or means of accomplishing the vision that will provide for equally desirable results? If you look off to a mountain top, which aspect of getting to the mountain top is essential? Is it acceptable or even feasible to walk there? Could you take a helicopter? Could you build a tunnel? Could you drive there?
- Which resources do you have available or at your disposal? Although it may be acceptable to drive to the mountain top, this task becomes much more difficult if you need to build both the road and the vehicle. Clearly, you need to understand the parameters

within which you are operating. What are the costs of getting there? Do you have enough money to do the things you want or need to? Do you have the technical experience to achieve what you are about to request that others try to accomplish? Are consultants available who can help fill in any gaps?

■ Have you envisioned at least one path of implementation when establishing a cost estimate for the project? It may not be the best path, but its mere existence will force you to think through the details of what you and others are about to embark on. You need to have a plan. Even though most plans are wrong at some level, they provide useful information to others for how you envisioned reaching your destination.

■ Is the projected business return on investment realistic? Are the strategic elements of the project necessary for meeting all projections, or can some benefit be obtained by an initial tactical solution?

■ Has the business made a value judgment about the vision? Have executives determined whether it will provide the desired return on investment? The return may be strategic in nature versus a direct financial result, but this point needs to be established upfront. Is this something that can be achieved? Is it something that can fail?

■ Can the project be broken up into stage-gated process? (Such an approach would allow for incremental investment and incremental directional changes.)

■ When does this project need to be achieved?

■ What have other projects done? Where have they succeeded or failed? Sometimes, the impact crater that another project created when it crash-landed may not be worth navigating due to built-in organizational resistance. Conversely, a project that has been wildly successful may have established a foundation that is worth leveraging.

■ Has the technology or business landscape changed in a manner that requires more challenging assumptions than are currently held?

■ Do you know how your vision is different from previous failures? Can anything can be learned from these failures? How is the vision similar to previous successes? Knowing this type of information can help sell your vision.

■ Which aspects of relationships and cardinality are important? Modeling aspects of the system or project can help you understand the nature of the vision you are attempting to establish. Once you have the domain objects (terms, items) established, you can begin to elucidate the relationships between the objects. This unraveling of connections helps you understand the cardinality of the objects and relationships. Knowing or approximating the number of various parts of the vision can help you clarify what some of the real issues are.

- Have others done similar things in the company or in other similar companies? Are reference sites available? Are documented experiences and best practices available? You need to understand the nature of the risks that you are about to embark on.
- Have you had successful projects in the past? Success breeds trust. You need to ensure that the business will succeed. A beautiful and technically pure architecture may give you warm fuzzy feelings, but if it does not address the business needs required, you will not be successful. Note that "required" is not the same as "desired."

All of these factors need to be contemplated when establishing a vision and strategic direction. You want to be able to engage others within the appropriate boundaries, allow them to begin internalizing the vision, and encourage them to add depth to the vision (see Figure 4-4). For areas with established boundaries that have little or no flexibility in the vision, ensure that you have documentation for others to reference with respect to those boundaries.

You cannot say yes to everything in an attempt to placate others and gain their buy-in. That is not leadership.

Engage Others Through Influence

The essential quality of a leader is the ability to engage others to willingly travel toward a vision. For those in the role of architect, the ability to coerce

Figure 4-4   Once the vision is established, allow others to help figure out how to get there.

or mandate a set path is limited. Architects are usually not managers, and those who are doing the work rarely report directly to them.

The best architects are also capable project managers in their own right, may be part of the corporate management team, or may manage a team of architects. Nevertheless, the key point about leadership is that the role should not rely on hierarchy, but on a shared vision of the truth regarding the right direction for a particular project solution. Consequently, the approach taken toward project execution needs to be based more on influence, where you work to engage others to begin internalizing the goals and vision you are attempting to establish.

Enable Others to Take Ownership

Don't tell people how to do things; tell them what to do and let them surprise you with their results.

—George S. Patton, U.S. General

One of the most effective ways to lead a transition from vision to project execution is to engage others in determining how things will be done. This process allows the project team to begin taking ownership of the ideas and bring them into reality. Slowly working toward transitioning the knowledge, rationale, and principles behind the decisions that went into establishing the vision into real-world work allows the project team to become immersed in the essence of what is trying to be accomplished.

Capturing decisions in a concrete form during this period is critical. This effort makes it easier for newcomers to blend into the existing team as they join the project.

As different areas of the organization begin to formulate their own mental models of the project, they can begin assuming more responsibility for the project's execution. Their ownership will also allow you, as the leader, to do other things while the team is executing the plan.

When you transfer as much domain knowledge as possible, team members can begin making decisions in your absence. As an architect, you simply cannot be everywhere at once. In some sense, you want the project team to be capable of executing the project with only minimal oversight from you. A sufficient depth of knowledge transfer allows you to implicitly influence even the smallest design decisions, which will be naturally aligned with the overall vision.

Clear documentation about your vision will increase the likelihood that the execution will be in accordance with your vision. The documents need to be available at multiple levels, starting with a simple presentation slide setting out the vision and principles in a particular area, backed up with a more detailed document that describes how to execute plans based on the principles and best practices and clearly states what the boundaries are.

Deal with Conflict

Leaders need to be able to deal with conflict. As a leader, you will find that conflict routinely arises and must be actively dealt with, rather than being allowed to fester. Your ability to resolve and redirect the conflict is critical. Often, what appears to be a conflict on the surface is really just violent agreement. If it is, recognize it as such and move forward. If there really is a conflict, consider the following:

1. Engage all involved parties (privately and individually if needed).
2. Listen to what is being said.
3. Find the root cause.
4. Restate your understanding of the problem in your own words as succinctly as possible.
5. Address the issue in a manner that clearly demonstrates that you understand the matter.
6. Seek to find a resolution that is palatable to the parties involved.
7. Maintain integrity with the vision you are trying to accomplish.

The second point in the list is actually the most important: Listen. Listening to the interested parties and restating your understanding of the problem is often therapeutic in itself, but listening to and understanding the points of view of all parties in a conflict is the key to effective mediation. The ability to mediate and resolve conflict is one of the hallmarks of a true leader.

SUMMARY

The road to becoming a great leader begins with the following guidelines:

- Leadership principles:
  - Establish trust.
  - Establish a common vision.
  - Establish strategic partnerships.
  - Eat your own dog food.

- ▪ Perceive risks, assessing their impact and acting to minimize them.
- ▪ Deal with risk appropriately.
- ▪ Leadership strategies:
  - ▪ Utilize Occam's Razor.
  - ▪ Present information in a visual format.
  - ▪ Lead by keeping things focused.
  - ▪ Look for opportunities to leverage existing resources.
  - ▪ Sell the vision based on the context of the audience.
  - ▪ Focus executives on strategy, not conflict resolution.
- ▪ Leadership timing:
  - ▪ Capitalize on organizational momentum.
  - ▪ Learn when to step in and rescue a project.
  - ▪ Know when to stand alone.
  - ▪ Know when to ask for forgiveness versus when to ask for permission.
- ▪ Leading others:
  - ▪ Engage others through influence.
  - ▪ Allow others to contribute.
  - ▪ Support others in taking ownership.
  - ▪ Deal with conflict.

The good news is that becoming a great leader is a skill that can be learned with persistence. It requires a passion for the direction that you want others to pursue. You truly need to believe in the vision. Being passionate about technology is usually not a challenge for most people in the technology field, but being willing to allow others to shape that vision and contribute to it is a totally different story.

Take the time to master one or two of the skills mentioned in this chapter at a time. Consciously evaluate your actions against what you are trying to accomplish. After a period of time, it will become a habit that is easily repeatable. You will quietly become the leader you are seeking to be.

BIBLIOGRAPHY

Burnett, Mark. (2005). *Jump In! Even if You Don't Know How to Swim*. Ballantine Books.

Citrin, James M.; Smith, Richard A. (2004). *The 5 Patterns of Extraordinary Careers: The Guide for Achieving Success and Satisfaction*. Crown Business.

Covey, Stephan R. (2000). *Principle Centered Leadership.* Simon & Schuster.

Covey, Stephan R. (2008). *The Speed of Trust: The One Thing That Changes Everything* [Audio CD]. Simon & Schuster Audio.

Kilts, James M.; Mandfredi, John F.; Lorber, Robert. (2007). *Doing What Matters: How to Get Results That Make a Difference: The Revolutionary Old-Fashioned Approach* [Audio CD]. Random House Audio.

Magee, David. (2004). *Ford Tough: Bill Ford and the Battle to Rebuild America's Automaker.* Wiley.

Maxwell, John C. (1995). *Developing the Leaders Around You: How to Help Others Reach Their Full Potential.* Thomas Nelson.

Maxwell, John C. (2000). *Fail Forward: Turning Mistakes into Stepping Stones for Success.* Thomas Nelson.

Maxwell, John C. (1998). *The 21 Irrefutable Laws of Leadership: Follow Them and People Will Follow.* Thomas Nelson.

Maxwell, John C. (2004). *Winning with People: Discover the People Principles That Work for You Every Time.* Thomas Nelson.

Nightingale, Earl. (1986). *Lead the Field.* Nightingale Conant.

Salka, John. (2004). *First In, Last Out: Leadership Lessons from the New York Fire Department.* Portfolio.

Schmitt, Bernd H. (2008). *Big Think Strategy: How to Leverage Bold Ideas and Leave Small Thinking Behind (Your Coach in a Box)* [Audio CD]. Your Coach Digital.

Chapter 5

POLITICS

Trust is always earned, never given.

—R. Williams

Politics are a very unsatisfactory game.

—Henry B. Adams

Nothing is so admirable in politics as a short memory.

—John Kenneth Galbraith

Most people cringe when they hear the term *politics*. They quickly recall some bad experience associated with politics and hope to avoid encountering the situation again at almost any cost.

Rarely do you encounter anyone who has a single good thing to say about politics. It is talked about with such passion that if you didn't know better, you would swear that politics was a very, very bad person. It is such a one-sided discussion that it begins to make your mind wonder: Is politics really the evil villain that it is portrayed to be?

Given the multifaceted nature of the role of an architect, the reality of politics comes into play on a daily basis from many different directions.

This chapter discusses the essence of politics as a soft skill for software architects.

POLITICS DEFINED

"Politics (from Greek πολιτικος, [politikós]: «citizen», «civilian»), is a process by which groups of people make collective decisions."[1]

---

1. "Politics." 2011. *Wikipedia*. Wikipedia Foundation. Retrieved June 15, 2011, from http://en.wikipedia.org/wiki/Politics.

The really short definition of politics is "the art of getting things done by collaborating with other people."

Key concepts: conflict, conflict resolution, self-interest, authority, misaligned goals, motives, approach, relationships, network (each person has his or her own), chits (political cash or debt), compromise, and culture.

The Political Marketplace

Nearly everything you do during the course of the day is a political financial transaction. To achieve a goal, you are spending, receiving, or borrowing political capital within your political network.

We regularly see the political systems that shape national and world interactions, but we sometimes fail to recognize that the same forces are at play in the typical business enterprise. Our interactions with other people where we provide assistance may be gaining us future collateral as an astute investment; alternatively, the way we work may be taking us into debt as we rely too much upon others for help.

Given this context, consider the following:

- Are you making investments?
- Are you serving only your own self-interests or purposes?
- Are you incurring political debt?
- Is the result you are seeking worth the price?
- Will all parties involved be happy with the transaction? Does it matter?
- If everyone is not happy who needs to be, what could be changed to satisfy their needs?
- Are you being strong-armed into a position? If so, why? And which alternatives do you have available?
- Is what is being done the right thing to do?
- Is what is being done technically correct?
- Is what is being done correct from a business point of view? If not, why not?
- Will the person who has lobbied so hard for a position stick to that position when it comes under scrutiny?
- Are you willing to defend the position when it comes under scrutiny? If not, why not?

For any given transaction, not all parties involved will view it as positive.

The realities in the political ecosystem need to be understood: Everyone has a history, a point of view on a particular subject based on that history, and an organizational context in which they operate that drives their motivations. The interplay between these different aspects of each individual in an organization and its hierarchy is what creates politics, and politics is part of being human. The people with whom you associate inevitably carry political baggage or aura/presence, so be aware of the positive or negative effects that they may have upon you and your points of view and context.

In many ways, the political system within your company is similar to the stock market. Things are constantly changing. Political power/influence ebbs and flows. The person or group that you have historically relied upon to help solidify a deal may suddenly be gone due to a reorganization or simply may have changed due to the current stresses and strains operating between people on an everyday basis. Play nice—the person you made unhappy may suddenly become your boss.

Unintended political consequences may be the result of our not fully seeing or being aware of the true financial, organizational, or personal costs of a particular decision. Think and act carefully and always maintain a 360° view of what is going on in the organization around you.

If human relationships are transactional and value based, politics is the business marketplace where social collateral is traded on a daily basis in an attempt to gain some other object of worth. The aim of most human social interactions is to increase our net worth and capital in this relationship currency for later spending.

The political marketplace is where you haggle over price, search for the right thing, and maybe join forces if your political account is running a bit low on funds. Before joining forces, however, you should step into the other person's shoes and see the world and the relationship you are entering into from his or her point of view; that perspective will help you determine whether you will be an equal partner and whether you will really get out of it what you expect. As always, "Caveat emptor" (Let the buyer beware).

In the political marketplace, you always need to be careful of what is being sold:

- Do you really understand what you are getting?
- What is the other person's motivation? (What does that person get in return?) This is a barter system.

- Will what you are doing likely come back to bite you?
- What are you not being told about?
- What are the weaknesses that are not being portrayed?
- What does your gut tell you about this situation? Gut feelings have a critical place in politics because politics is all about people; your subconscious senses many things that can legitimately give you a positive or negative feeling.
- Are you paying a fair price or are you helping build out some infrastructure?
- What are the strategic efforts that are being pursued? Is what you are being asked to do in alignment with the strategic direction?

Be careful of people who do not stand behind what they say when the heat turns up. Watch. Listen. Observe. People rarely change their behavior. They are likely to repeat it over and over again.

The best way to play the game of politics is to not play at all:

- Treat people with respect.
- Be known for dealing honestly in facts.
- Don't take advantage of people when they are down.
- Show integrity in all interactions.
- If you say you are going to do something, do it.
- Recognize that your word is your honor; it represents who you are.

These guidelines may sound like the basic rules you heard in kindergarten, but they bear repeating. Unfortunately, many people are held back in their careers because they lack these key soft skills.

Unfortunately, not everyone is going to be happy all of the time. You will need to make hard decisions. The effects of those decisions may not always be clear, however. You need to make the best decision (political expenditure) you can with the information you have and then jump. Don't be afraid to ask for what you really want—you might actually get it. Later, if necessary, adjustments can be made to account for new circumstances or realized circumstances.

When I think about politics as being the art of getting things done and the first four chapters, I think of the following equation:

Success at Politics = Gracious Behavior + Communication +
Negotiation + Leadership

By applying the principles discussed earlier, you will gain a solid foundation for being effective at politics.

Many people consider the game of politics to have a negative connotation. They consider it to be an area where people are shading the truth, operating solely for their own self-centered purposes, not disclosing critical information, or potentially operating directly against others' interests. Although these types of things may, in fact, happen, I want to believe they are the exception and not the rule.

Politics is about dealing with people and relationships. Any interaction with a group of people involves some sort of politics at some level. What makes politics positive or negative comes down to how we engage in it—not just what level of success we achieve.

This chapter discusses the four key aspects of engaging in the political marketplace (see Figure 5-1):

- Political context (understanding the environment you are operating in)
- Political principles (your personal rules of engagement)
- Political strategies (how to approach engaging in the political marketplace)
- Political timing (when to engage)

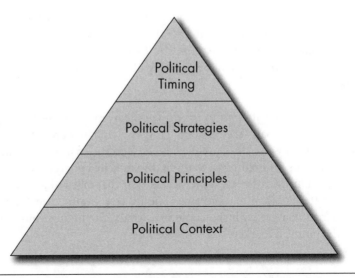

Figure 5-1   Four key aspects of engaging in the political marketplace

POLITICAL CONTEXT

One of the most important things you can do as an architect is to understand the political context of the environment you are working in. In a real sense, it lets you know where you are within multiple contexts within the business. Understanding the context simplifies your decision making and guides you in establishing a politically viable vision for your projects.

Align with Strategic Company Directions

For architects, being aware of the political environment is critical for success. This means knowing the following:

- Where is the company trying to go strategically? (Is it moving into a new business sector? Is it trying to build up a particular product line?)
- Who are your chief competitors?
- Which kinds of technology is your competition using?
- What are the key areas of focus for research and development?
- How does your company make money?
- Which areas are being invested in?
- Which kinds of acquisitions are being made?
- Which kinds of divestitures are being made?

Although this kind of information is more business related, it directly affects how and where the company is interested in investing its money.

Every dollar the company spends on you and your projects needs to return money back to the company from now through the foreseeable future. As a result, any money that you seek needs to be requested wisely. This is best done if you can sell the decision by pointing out how it aligns with key business objectives.

In general, you should attempt to maximize the overlap between your goals and the company's goals (see Figure 5-2). If you find any areas that do not match the company's goals, closely evaluate them to ensure that you have very good reasons for holding onto them. Mismatched goals may cause you a long series of justifications and political battles that may reduce your overall value in the political marketplace. The inverse is also true: The more closely aligned you are with the company's goals, the higher your implicit value in the political marketplace will likely be.

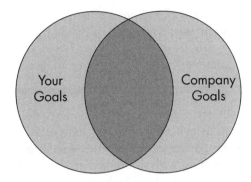

Figure 5-2 Maximize overlap between your goals and the company's goals.

Key Point
From a political perspective, you need to ensure that your goals are aligned with the company's goals.

Understand the Cultural Context That Surrounds You

The cultural differences that exist from group to group can influence the approach that is needed to be successful in navigating the political waters for that group. Perhaps their processes follow more of a documentation-centric waterfall model versus a more lightweight agile model. Some groups are consensus driven, whereas others are authoritatively driven, such that a single individual is the source for decisions.

Cultural differences may arise based on the physical location of the offices that the individuals occupy. This factor can affect how direct you need to be in your approach. It can also affect how responses should be interpreted. Does yes mean, "Yes, I understand what you are saying," or "Yes, we are in agreement"?

In some cultures, admitting you are wrong or have made a mistake is just not done. In some, saying you do not understand something is frowned upon.

When you are on a project, ask yourself: Are the resources for the project local or remote? Are the resources primarily employees or contractors?

Taking the time to understand the variations in cultural norms can help you avoid political landmines. At the end of the day, you need to strive for clarity, both in what you are communicating (Does your audience truly understand what you are saying?) and what you are hearing (Do you truly understand what the others are saying?).

Getting to a point where you share a common understanding of the assumptions, risks, and issues associated with a particular set of decisions is essential to ensuring the long-term success of those decisions. The less familiar you are with the individuals with whom you are interacting or the farther you are physically from those individuals, the more you should focus on slowing down and moving through the decision-making process more deliberately.

You are far better off making good decisions slowly than poor decisions quickly. Once perceived agreements have been reached, extricating yourself from those decisions due to a lack of common understanding of exactly what was agreed upon can be tricky.

Take time to document what was decided, who was involved, which assumptions were made, what was included, and what was excluded. A few weeks or a few months later, everyone's recollections of exactly what was decided can become a bit cloudy. A greater distance between parties, either organizationally or physically, will necessitate being more formal with your approach around reaching decisions.

Address Others' Concerns Early

As an architect, you will hear an endless stream of concerns from nearly every direction, each with its own context. Although every concern and issue bears a different weight with respect to the impact it may have on the organization as a whole, your ability to manage or soften the collateral damage surrounding the issue often is in direct proportion to ability to deal with the issue quickly.

The more you let things fester on their own with no attention, the more you allow the issue to take on a personality of its own, and the more you allow it be cast in the light selected by those raising the concern.

Each time someone affected by the perceived issue discusses it with someone else, the pool of disengaged individuals potentially grows. Over time, a cascade effect may cause the issue to appear bigger than it is. The more the issue is allowed to grow on its own, the greater the effort required to bring it back under containment.

The political impacts of not managing issues swiftly can be large. If it is something trivial, executives will wonder why you let this concern drift up to them and did not manage it yourself. If it is something significant (your hardware estimates are off by a million dollars), the executives will want to know why you didn't drop everything, bring the problem to their attention immediately, and deliver the message personally. Whatever the impact of the issue, the key response needed to avoid executive backlash and ruined career prospects is simply to address the issue quickly before it gets out of control and takes on a life of its own.

The challenge with addressing other people's concerns is that you cannot be everywhere at once, you cannot do everything at once, and there is simply more work than you can possibly do in a day. Knowing which balls you can drop is an important skill to acquire. As an architect, you will be asked to juggle many balls simultaneously. Quickly assessing which balls will break and which balls will bounce when they have been dropped is critical.

To be successful, you need to develop an internal sense of priority and potential impact for everything that comes your way. You need to learn to do the following:

- Quickly shift context. (Push what you were previously thinking about onto your internal stack to deal with later.)
- Focus on what is directly in front of you.
- Listen for what is being said (and for what is not being said).
- Ask questions that will bring you to clarity.
- Seek to understand what is being said.
- Get to the root cause.
- Think.
- Determine a reasonable path for what needs to happen next.
- If you can resolve the issue now, do it.
- If you need to inform an executive, do it once you have identified at least three alternatives and have a preference for which of the three is recommended.
- If you believe the issue can be left to its own devices, let it go (be careful with these decisions—they have a habit of coming back to bite you).
- Make sure you have expressed clearly to your boss why you have decided to let the issue remain unaddressed to avoid the perception of incompetence.

Although context switching to address issues quickly comes at a price (lost focus that you will need to regain to return to the task you were working on), prioritization and accurate assessment of the impact of an issue, followed by a quick resolution, is a key political skill for an architect. This skill often distinguishes an average architect from a great one.

Believe in What You Are Selling

In the world of politics and architecture, you are perennially selling things. So many things always need to be done, and a certain level of sales skill is always required to obtain commitments for getting someone else to do a particular task.

You may not always be passionate about what you are selling during the normal daily grind, but you do need to believe in what you request of others. If we aren't motivated and engaged in a task, how can we ask someone else to do it? Your body language and tone of voice will give away the value you place on that task.

You may need to think through the task from multiple perspectives to determine exactly why what you are requesting is important. You need to understand its context to be successful at the sale. Consider these questions:

- What value does the business receive from this task being done?
- Which strategic direction is being met by doing this task?
- Which risk is being avoided?
- Which costs are being avoided?
- How will this task make supporting or maintaining the system easier?
- Which revenue gains will be supported?
- Which new technology will the person who performs the task get to learn?
- How will this improve customers' experience with your product?

If you really don't believe in what you are selling, why does it need to be done? Maybe it doesn't need to be done, or maybe it can be done differently in a way that will gain your own personal buy-in.

Don't ask others to do things you do not believe in or are not willing to do yourself. If you as the architect don't believe in the task given your unique position of understanding the scope of project and its solution, then is the task truly necessary?

Not My Problem

When I look around, I always see things that I would not have done the same way as someone else. I have an opinion, but unless someone directly asks, I try to keep it to myself. Others are working hard to do the right thing, and I am likely not aware of the set of circumstances (the political context) surrounding the decisions that were or are being made. Let others live in peace. Your wise words of wisdom about something you don't completely understand may not be well received, and later when you need help on something else, those individuals' interest level in helping you (your number of chits available) may be a bit low.

I refer to this situation as NMP (not my problem). I can't fix all of the world's problems. Others are certainly capable and will do an excellent job in dealing with the issues in front on them. In short, you may want to give other people a subtle head's up, but don't stick your nose where it doesn't belong and is likely not all that welcome.

Conversely, if someone asks for your opinion, feel free to share what you feel is appropriate and remember to be both gracious and discrete. You may be commenting on something that may not be a work of art to you, but is precious to that person.

Relationships (Context with Others) Matter

When you really, really need to get something done and it is extremely important to you, it is unlikely that you will be able to get that task done completely on your own. Instead, you will likely need to draw in other people to help you get the job completed in the time frame available. Your ability to accomplish this goal will likely depend on the relationships you have formed with others.

Have you taken the time to eat lunch with your coworkers, pitch in and help them out when they had a problem that needed attention, or just stop by to talk (not about work-related items)? Asking others in the office how they're doing and really listening to their responses engenders good will.

In the world of politics, the people you know and with whom you have taken time to forge relationships can have a dramatic impact on your ability to pursue your agenda (your goals).

You need to forge relationships with a few people who can give you honest feedback. Then, when you are acting poorly, they can let you know that what you may innocently be doing is offending others, and that you should look to adjust your behavior.

If you find yourself talking about someone else or that person's behavior, stop and think, "Is this really the best use of my time? Am I really trying to help out the person we are talking about? Would I feel comfortable if that person were here to hear the conversation firsthand?" If the answer is no to any of these questions, change the subject.

Afterward, if you feel comfortable that you can bring up the topic in a non-confrontational and gracious manner, take the time to talk to the person who was the center of the previous conversation and let him know how his behavior is being perceived. He will likely be uncomfortable, but will appreciate the feedback.

In the end, you should focus on having a positive relationship with everyone (even those people who drive you completely nuts). This will enable you to regularly have better days and feel better about yourself.

POLITICAL PRINCIPLES

To be effective in a sustainable manner within the world of politics, you need to ground yourself with a core set of principles (see Figure 5-3). These

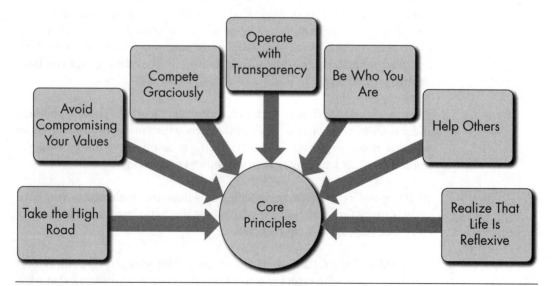

Figure 5-3 Core principles to adopt for the political marketplace

principles can act as a solid rudder for guiding your decisions and give you a consistency in your decision making that will help establish and increase others' trust in you.

Taking the High Road

Sometimes in the heat of the battle, politics appears to be playing a key role. In this situation, it is tempting and possibly even fun to contemplate just jumping in and responding in kind.

It has been my experience that no matter what you choose to do for perceived political reasons, responding in kind rarely leads to the desired results. If the politics involved was as you perceived, you are likely just inviting a worse response than the first event. If you misinterpreted what was done and why it was done, you will likely find yourself trying to explain—to those people to whom you would prefer to project a positive image—how you (normally the cool, calm, well-mannered, and sane individual) could have possibly reacted in such an irrational manner.

Instead, choose to assume the best possible intentions of those involved and take the high road when you are responding to things during the course of the day. At best, you will be held in a positive regard by those around you. At worst, you will avoid looking extremely foolish.

Avoid Compromising Your Values

The daily political pressures of getting things done on time and on budget with limited resources can easily push you toward expediency. You need to have a clear understanding of what your values are and what your boundaries are. You don't want to extend yourself across a boundary where you cannot compromise without feeling a sense of personal loss.

Some boundaries are clear: moral boundaries, company policies, and state and federal laws, for example.

Other areas are not as clear. How much overtime can you work without significantly affecting your family? How much work do you bring home at night?

To help keep your sanity and to be able to go home at night feeling good about what you do, take the time to think through your values and adhere to them as best you can.

Compete Graciously

The world of politics is filled with competition. Your ideas, projects, and capabilities are constantly being compared to and contrasted with those of others. Only a few will survive, and you need to be willing to step into the ring, take a few punches, and give a few punches. That doesn't mean you should fight dirty so you can win. Instead, it means you should execute your tasks with integrity and graciousness.

Companies want people who have some drive within them. They want individuals who can take a few knocks, get up, and keep going. They want persistence. They want workers who believe in what they are doing. They want employees who know where they are going. They want leaders who have some vision even when it's cloudy and rainy.

The way to compete graciously is to be open and honest, act with integrity, listen to other people's ideas, and treat others and their proposals with respect. If you behave well with others, those individuals in turn will be more likely to treat you and your ideas graciously. This approach doesn't mean you ignore issues, but when you point them out, you do so in a neutral and factual manner without malice or scorn. Treat others the way you would have them treat you.

Operate with Transparency

You disarm others when you are transparent. Others' ability to influence your decision based on disclosure of a particular matter is removed. Transparency also allows you to operate more freely in your own thinking—after all, you have nothing to hide.

One way to accomplish this goal is to document each architectural decision with the reasoning that underpins it and the alternatives considered but not selected. Ensure that this document is available for all to see.

If the reasoning is clear, most challenges will fall away or come down to matters of opinion rather than facts. This outcome will support leaving decisions intact and reduce unfavorable politics.

Be Who You Are

Sometimes during the course of events, you may be tempted to present yourself as something you are not simply for the sake of expediency. Although this may be effective for a short period of time, it is not a sustainable strategy. You cannot be everything to everyone.

You need to figure out who you are, what you want to be, and where you want to go. Perhaps there are specific areas in which you want to grow and actively improve specific skills, but you are unlikely to holistically change fundamentally who you are.

Be who you are—the best, most authentic person you can be.

Help Others and Don't Expect Anything in Return

When you help someone out, give that assistance with a mindset of no strings attached; assume that your action is simply an act of goodwill. Don't do it with the mindset of "You will owe me in the future." Other people will see through your intentions and perceive you as shallow. You may then be labeled with the reputation of being a politician—someone who will say and do anything to get what she wants.

Be genuine in all your interactions, and others will be more likely to be genuine with you. Give praise where it is deserved. Listen to people. All of these small steps build trust.

Realize That Life Is Reflexive

In the world of politics, not everything is fair. Many of the factors that surround you are simply out of your control. Even so, you can tilt things in your favor by realizing one simple fact: Life is reflexive. That is, what you project out is reflected back to you. When you think about it, you choose how the world will treat you by how you treat it.

If someone says something that seems hurtful, personal, or just downright mean, you rarely have the context to understand or fully interpret the actions or thoughts of others. Take a bold step and assume that the person means the best and that the remark simply didn't come across as intended. Even if the message was intended to be harmful, you will personally be better off if you choose to respond kindly instead of in kind.

In challenging situations, if you are able to keep your cool and behave in a gracious manner, your composure will be noticed. The people with the power to promote you will likely notice that you are not only technically capable, but also socially capable even under duress. Grace under fire or in defeat usually earns the respect of others. It will help establish trust, which is a critical factor when interacting with executives and others.

Although others may be choosing to play "politics as usual," avoid wading into these murky waters and instead play your own game—the one where you choose how to respond and the actions you wish to pursue. Most of the challenges we face can be viewed as tests to see what we have learned. If we fail, we will probably have to retake the test.

After a while, the things that used to drive us nuts, and to which we consciously had to choose to respond graciously, begin to fade as the behavior of graciousness becomes a habit. By choosing to embrace the reflexivity of life, you can be reasonably happy even when political storms abound, because you are in control of how you choose to respond, regardless of the circumstances.

POLITICAL STRATEGIES

A variety of approaches can help you be effective politically simply by adopting a strategy and using it at the appropriate times. In some sense, you could think of these strategies as political design patterns.

Help Others Achieve Their Objectives

When you see someone struggling with a problem (even an individual whom you don't particularly like), step in and lend a helping hand. You may not have the time to completely solve the problem, but you can help her get over a hurdle or two.

These little things add up over time. You are building up a set of goodwill (chits) that later will engender others to want to help you out when you are having your own struggles.

These little things help you get to know other people better and make your own day seem sunnier.

Learn to Enjoy the Journey (Not Just the Destination)

When you consider projects and requests that are of a truly high priority, it is easy to become consumed with the prospect of arriving at the destination at all costs. The problem when we do so is that we push aside other projects, other people's concerns, and march doggedly toward the goal. Unfortunately, this laser-like focus on achieving the goal often leaves a wake of carnage behind us. Although we may get to the destination on time and on budget, the number of people left with bruised feelings could be potentially high.

Slowing down a bit and bringing people along for the ride (versus driving over them) will help build valuable relationships. Learn to enjoy the challenges and the collaborative efforts it takes to accomplish things as partners. Do little things for others, like saying thank you, buying a gift card to Caribou Coffee, directing interesting problems their way, asking for their opinion on how to approach a problem, and so on. These small gestures will help make each day more enjoyable.

Strive for Excellence in the Areas That Matter

When you are working on your pet project, it is easy to fall into the pitfall of polishing, redoing, and continually refining your work of art. It's fun. It feels soooo good. Nearly everyone will be impressed with the sheer brilliance behind your latest creation.

Although this kind of goldplating is fun, is it really the best use of your time in an extremely busy day and when many other priorities are waiting for your attention? Your task may be to produce a world-class masterpiece, but my guess is that it is not. Ask yourself: Is it good enough?

We do need to strive for excellence, but really only to the degree that it will benefit the company in a meaningful way. When you measure the risks and rewards from your company's perspective, would you do what you are doing if you owned the company and you were paying for the work that you are currently diligently engaging in?

From a political perspective, perception is everything. You need to be perceived as someone who adds significant value to the company, not as someone who squanders valuable resources.

As you progress through your day's activities, keep in mind that sometimes good enough is well enough. You don't need to solve all of the world's problems, so don't try to boil the ocean. Do what needs to be done, do it well, and proceed to the next highest-priority item.

Be Willing to Compromise on Lower-Priority Goals

When you are attempting to get things done or to achieve a particular goal, know in advance what is truly important to you. If you give in on the one item that you were truly passionate about, you may lose all of your motivation to accomplish what you set out to do. It may leave you with an empty feeling that produces a string of poor decisions to follow.

A string of poor decisions could begin framing a public perception by others that you are not all that talented and maybe should not be in your current position. Your political clout may be reduced (or your number of chits in the game reduced), even though you really did not get a chance to spend it on something more valuable—you simply gave your power away.

Before reacting to the compromise, make sure you understand the reason why you were so passionate about the item. Was it the technology, the approach, or the potential benefits? Use this understanding when weighing other decisions, and make sure your passion has some fact-based balance to use as a measure.

If some level of compromise was required regarding the item you were most passionate about, try to maintain a positive attitude by using your earlier measure to examine the effect of the change and to look at other decisions. This more positive and measured approach will not just improve other decisions, but will also make living with compromised decisions and the effect on your working life and self-esteem a lot easier to cope with.

Don't Take Offense to Poor Behavior

Have you ever been traveling along the course of a perfect day, when suddenly out of nowhere someone says something or does something that is simply offensive? Your first natural responses may be either fight (respond with a cutting remark: "What kind of idiot are you?") or flight (respond with nothing, exit stage door left, and brood over the scene that just played out).

Unfortunately, time is a funny matter. Once it has passed, there is no going back—the cement has set. No matter what you do, and no matter how hard you try, whatever has happened to you simply cannot be undone. It may be remedied—compensation of some sort may be provided—but it is now simply a fixture of history.

At this point, choosing to be offended by what just happened will not do you any favors; it can affect nearly every aspect of your personality, and most likely not in a positive manner. Instead, choose to forgive the person and ignore the bad behavior rather than respond. That approach will make you more relaxed and give you the high ground in the future; it will also likely deflate the offender and defuse the situation. This outcome is far better than creating a situation that rapidly escalates.

Depending on the nature of what just occurred, you may choose to respond in any number of ways. If this is the first time, you may want to simply let it pass by. If the offense breaks a law or company policy, you may want to get the appropriate authorities involved. If it falls somewhere in between these two extremes, you may want to talk to the person directly—once you have had a chance to regain your composure—and let him know that his actions or words were neither acceptable nor appreciated.

If the person chooses to apologize, accept the apology. Whether he apologizes or not, forgive him, learn whatever you can glean from the matter, put it behind you, and move on.

Confront Interpersonal Issues Privately

If you believe someone is working directly in opposition to you or has said some negative things about you, you may want to talk to the person privately. Find out what she really said—sometimes a message that has traveled a long distance has changed its content and no longer represents what was really said. Often the context in which a statement is made can completely change its meaning, so take time to understand that context.

If someone said something that truly offended you, talk to her privately. On the one hand, the remark may not have been intended the way you perceive it. It may have a different interpretation. On the other hand, it may truly have been stated the way it appeared, and the person may apologize for it. If she doesn't apologize, forgive her and forget about it. You will likely need to work with the individual in the future, and it will be easier to cooperate if you are not carrying a chip on your shoulder.

POLITICAL TIMING

Learning to be effective in a political environment requires you to develop a sense of timing of when it is best to pursue certain avenues versus when the right course is to simply drop the matter and let it pass.

Timing in the political marketplace is essential. If your timing is wrong, you will grind the gears of the political marketplace and cause political friction that may be completely unnecessary and draw significant, and unwanted, attention to yourself. Conversely, if your timing is correct, you will interact with the political marketplace like well-timed gears—in a powerful and nearly frictionless manner (see Figure 5-4).

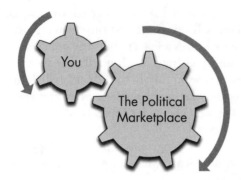

Figure 5-4 Develop a sense of timing within the political marketplace.

Execute Things in a Timely Fashion

Often, you may hear people talk about how the current political environment (e.g., the set of current strategic directions, financial circumstances, leadership structure, organizational clout [chits]) influences the decisions being made.

In the context of the current political environment, once you achieve a consensus and secure commitments from everyone on a particular course of action, it is important to execute that action quickly. Political circumstances can change rapidly, causing what were once firm commitments to a particular course of action to evaporate.

Once a decision begins to be executed, the organizational momentum to complete things becomes strong, and everyone is likely to stand behind their commitments. However, as time proceeds, if dates are missed or the budget is exceeded (a storm in the political environment), the organizational willpower to carry through the decision may come to an end. To avoid this kind of waffling, focus on timely delivery of projects.

Helping project managers to actively manage budgets, scope, deadlines, and resources will enable the team to execute things in a timely fashion and help maintain a friendly political environment.

Don't ask for cross-organizational commitments too early. You are just setting things up for failure if the political environment changes in the future.

On the flip side, you may want to seek early commitments to ensure that your interests have time to be prioritized early on, when resources may be plentiful. As the saying goes, the early bird gets the worm.

As with most things of a political nature, learning to listen to your gut will give you a sense of what is appropriate for timing and seeking commitments.

Failure Today Does Not Mean You Will Not Succeed Tomorrow

Failure is an opportunity to learn what does not work. In my experience, the first time you encounter a problem, you rarely understand the essence of the true challenge involved. It is only through dogged persistence of looking, trying, retreating, and retrying to solve a problem that you begin to understand the nature of the problem (as the saying goes, experience is the best teacher).

If you look back at nearly any project or task, you will see many mini-failures that needed to be overcome. You needed to put your chin forward and run into the brick wall a few times before you were able to break through, overcome, or go around the obstacle.

From the outside, people will see your end success, but they rarely see the sweat and toil that got you there. When they talk to you, they will be amazed at the volume of knowledge you seem to so easily possess and convey. What they may not realize is the personal cost that you paid for each grain of knowledge.

The main thing to remember is that failure is a large part of success. Don't get discouraged when things aren't going your way. Success is usually just around the corner from discouragement. Dogged persistence will get you to where you want to be, but you really need to want that goal and be willing to pay the price to get there.

Learn to smile and be lighthearted about the times when things didn't go your way. It will make you more fun to be around and make people more interested in working with you on the next project.

Realize That Politically, You Will Not Always Win

Sometimes, a goal is so important to you that you can hardly think of a single other concept. Every action, every thought, is focused on pursuing that goal. It seems that sometimes the more stridently you pursue the goal, the more intimidating the barriers become as you move closer to it.

When the day comes that the goal (at least temporarily) was not achieved, it can bring an immense amount of frustration and disappointment. You may be tempted to blame others (especially those who were, of course, not politically aligned with your goal), mope around, and generally be an unpleasant companion.

If possible, consider the circumstance to represent a temporary setback and keep a good attitude. You are much more likely to be perceived by others in a positive fashion if you can raise your head and continue to be a productive member of the team.

My experience has been that when I take the focus off doggedly pursuing a goal, forgive others for the temporary roadblocks they seem to have unintentionally set before me, and go about enjoying the current day, my ability to have fun goes up dramatically and the goal I was chasing sometimes surprisingly shows up at my doorstep.

Get in the Game

As you move up in the organization, your need for well-honed soft skills increases, and the degree to which you rely solely on technical skills decreases.

Don't avoid situations or a position just because you perceive politics to be part of the role. Politics are a part of everyday life. You need to learn how to jump into tough situations and still relate to others in a positive manner.

Developing these skills may require you to go to some classes, read some books, and take a few risks. If you are like me, entering the realm of politics will move you out of your comfort zone and force you to grow. It may not always seem "fun," but you will enjoy the personal growth over time.

Learning how to play the game of politics is not as hard as it seems. You may get a few bumps and bruises along the way, but you will come out stronger in the end.

As you become a person skilled at politics, the combination of your great technical skills and your newfound soft skills will enable you to get great things done, feel good about yourself, and have fun along the journey.

So, jump in and get in the game—it's waiting for you.

BECOMING A GOOD POLITICIAN

The road to becoming a good politician begins with the following steps:

- Understanding what politics is.
- Understanding the nature of the political marketplace.
- Political context:
    - Align your goals with strategic company directions.
    - Understand the culture of where you are at.
    - Address the concerns of others early on.
    - Believe in what you are selling.
    - Realize that some things are not your problem.
    - Recognize that relationships matter.
- Political principles:
    - Take the high road.
    - Avoid compromising your values.
    - Compete graciously.
    - Operate with transparency.
    - Be who you are.
    - Help others and do not expect anything in return.
    - Realize that life is reflexive.
- Political strategies:
    - Help others achieve their objectives.
    - Learn to enjoy the journey and not just the destination.
    - Strive for excellence in the areas that matter.
    - Be willing to compromise on lower-priority goals.
    - Don't be offended by poor behavior.
    - Deal with interpersonal issues privately.
- Political timing:
    - Execute things in a timely fashion.
    - Realize that failure today does not preclude success tomorrow.
    - Realize that you will not always win.
    - Get in the game.

Politics is not always fun to deal with, but the techniques listed here are ways of working within the political system that will allow you to operate effectively on your own terms and maintain your sanity. For architects, the simple matter is that politics are unavoidable. You need to learn how to operate within the political realities of the company you work in.

BIBLIOGRAPHY

Bick, Julie. (1997). *All I Really Need To Know in Business I Learned at Microsoft.* Simon & Schuster.

Covey, Stephan R. (2008). *The Speed of Trust: The One Thing That Changes Everything* [Audio CD]. Simon & Schuster Audio.

Maxwell, John C. (2004). *Winning with People: Discover the People Principles that Work for You Every Time.* Thomas Nelson.

Swell, Marc T.; Sewell, Laura M. (2002). *The Software Architect's Profession: An Introduction.* Prentice Hall.

Part II

Personal Skills

If you can master yourself, you can master anything.

—Ancient Proverb

This part focuses on the three essential personal skills for an architect. The next three chapters address the key elements needed to become more effective in managing yourself as an architect:

- **Chapter 6: Transparency.** Your ability to operate and interact with other people, and to have all of the cards on the table, face up.
- **Chapter 7: Passion.** Your ability to fully engage in what you are doing.
- **Chapter 8: Context Switching.** Your ability to quickly and effectively refocus your attention at a moment's notice to a new context.

Personal skills are the second foundational layer of the soft skills needed to be an architect (see Figure P2-1 on the next page).

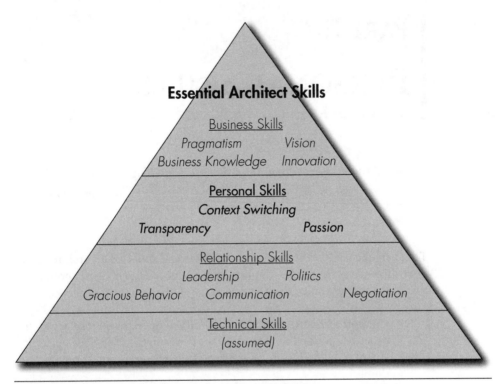

Figure P2-1   Essential architect skills: personal skills

Chapter 6

TRANSPARENCY

There is no persuasiveness more effectual than the transparency of a single heart, of a sincere life.

—Joseph Barber Lightfoot, English Theologian

When you are working with people in a corporate environment, your natural reaction is to want to put your best foot forward, to look as if you can solve all your problems independently, and to keep any issues tucked in your back pocket—"No problems here." Other areas and people with whom you interact may also wish to keep any issues they may have hidden from view.

The things that you and others fail to disclose are potential landmines for any project's ability to succeed. They will erode trust and hinder your ability to continue advancing up the corporate ladder.

This chapter shows how transparency can be used as a key soft skill to enable success as a software architect.

ARCHITECTS LIVE IN A GLASS HOUSE

Whether you are prepared for it or not, as you move into your new role as an architect, you are moving into a glass house. When you are in this position, your weaknesses and strengths become plainly visible for others to see.

All of your actions are played out on a public stage. Your results are impactful enough to the business that they are visible to nearly everyone in the local vicinity. Sometimes, it may seem like the position magnifies all of your imperfections.

If this idea doesn't make you feel humble, it should. You are about to enter (or have already entered) an arena where you are not the expert at everything. You will be asked to jump into new areas that you have not previously dealt with, and you will likely have very little time to prepare. You will need to learn and think on your feet. Others will get to watch you stumble, get up, brush off the dust, and move on.

After a while, you will learn to accept that when you are faced with never-before-encountered challenges, fear is not all bad. It is actually a good thing. It signals that your body is preparing for the new challenge.

As you learn about what needs to be done, follow these guidelines:

- Formulate a strategy for how to represent the information you have acquired.
- Identify the outstanding issues.
- Identify the assumptions that you are making.
- Validate the direction with others.
- Think through how you can solve the problem.
- Estimate the size of the problem.
- Estimate how much hardware is needed.
- Determine which groups need to be involved.
- Understand the concerns of each group.
- Capture areas of concern for which you may not have a solution.
- Document your reasons, your decisions, the alternatives, and the issues behind key decisions.

All of these steps speak to transparency: Issues are okay, assumptions are okay, documenting sizing information (even if it's just based on gut feel) is okay. The key is to bring clarity.

To allow others to begin understanding the nature of the problem, you must bring clarity through transparency—not only for yourself, but for others. Guess what: They may have the solution to a particular issue. Or perhaps they have the experience needed to know that an assumption that you are making is false—and they understand how to correct that assumption, or at least show how it should be an issue rather than an assumption.

When you build a transparent vision of where you want to go, the business can begin assessing risks, and everyone can begin assessing the likelihood of success. The nature of the problem can be fully addressed: Is this something we have done before? Is this something another company has done before (and maybe our organization should consider buying that company)? This information needs to be brought into clarity.

TYPES OF TRANSPARENCY

Architects need to be fluent in three types of transparency (see Figure 6-1):

- **Self-transparency.** This is transparency about you.
- **Project transparency.** This is transparency about your projects.
- **Relational transparency.** This is transparency about or from others.

SELF-TRANSPARENCY

Self-transparency includes areas such as being yourself, acknowledging your weaknesses, acknowledging your strengths and interests, and beating the crowd to your boss. The key concept here is to not hide who you are, but rather to be open about who you are. At first, this approach may seem challenging when you want to put your best foot forward. Nevertheless, you will establish trust with people in a more concrete manner by establishing transparency about yourself to others, including your boss.

Be Yourself

The best you can be at any given moment is yourself.

—Elizabeth Alraune

In nearly any setting, being yourself provides a level of authenticity that is compelling. No one expects you to be perfect. Your brand of humor, your style, and your likes and dislikes are things that are not easily hidden—so don't try to conceal them. People generally will appreciate and learn to like

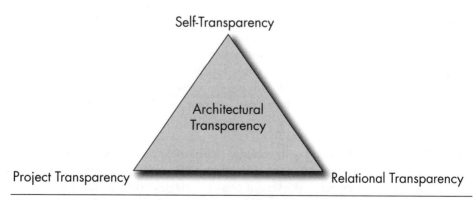

Figure 6-1   Three types of transparency—self-transparency, project transparency, and relational transparency—are the basis for architectural transparency.

you best when you are open and let them see the real you. Your natural tendencies should be expressed, yet tempered with the requirements of your role.

Later, if you have masqueraded as someone you are not, people will be surprised to find out who you really are. They may be a bit put off that you did not trust them enough to let them know who you truly were. They may also begin wondering what other things you may be hiding. In general, being yourself will build trust with others and will be sustainable. If you are just acting, eventually you will tire of the charade and want to be yourself.

No matter how badly you may want a particular promotion or a particular project, the process to getting there is best served when you are simply yourself. You provide unique insights and capabilities that are yours and yours alone. If you are not a good fit for the position, it is usually best if you don't get it; just be patient and wait for another opportunity to show your talent. If you are a good fit for the position, the things you have said and done to sell yourself as a good fit for the position will be assumptions of those who hired you: They expect you to be able to do at least what you claimed, and usually much more.

You need to have an internal passion about what you want to do. Later, when the excitement has worn off about the new position and it turns into more of a daily grind, you will need to have that internal passion for what you are doing to propel you forward even when the energy level is a bit lower or the politics seem a bit overwhelming.

Acknowledge Your Weaknesses

If there are things that you need to work on or technologies you are not fully up to speed on, be willing to share that information so that both your expectations and others' expectations for how a particular project will proceed are on the same page. Of course, your lack of knowledge doesn't absolve you of your responsibility to work and study to transform your weaknesses into strengths or, at a minimum, to build skills to a level that minimizes any negative impact. State that these areas are "current" weaknesses that you will work on.

You don't need to travel around with a sandwich board declaring your inadequate knowledge. When you are open about your weaknesses, you have the opportunity to seek training in the way of books or classes, to seek mentoring, or to hire contractors to come in and help.

For project managers, the acknowledgment of a knowledge gap in a certain area will give them an understanding that the schedule needs to start a bit slower, owing to the need to incorporate the new technology into the architectural stack. It may be an indicator that a proof of concept is required to prove out any potential capabilities that this technology may be able to provide. This step allows the technology to be vetted prior to the masses adopting this latest and greatest silver bullet that is promised to solve all technological problems and shorten project schedules from weeks or months to mere days.

Learn from the proof of concept and investigate best practices seen at other companies, possibly by seeking out vendor-independent reference sites. Also, make sure that adequate support and maintenance are available for the technology's use in the company for the future. If you aren't familiar with the technology as an architect and need help, it is also possible that others in the company will need help; it is the responsibility of the architect to ensure the project manager makes adequate arrangements for this "industrialization."

If you have some issues with time management and make others aware of that fact, they can be aware that you may need some additional follow-up to ensure things get done. Knowing that you are working to improve yourself will encourage others to give you a few breaks while you learn. Don't abuse this learning time by trying to do too much all at once—the latitude others will give for learning over delivery won't last long and your colleagues won't continue to carry you as dead weight. Instead, balance your learning with delivery and, in turn, offer to support your colleagues while they learn.

If you don't let others know your weaknesses, they may assume you are competent in certain areas. If so, when things start to unravel, they will not be pleased and will likely not be as forgiving that you failed to disclose something that is now a major problem for the project.

The key is to operate with transparency both with yourself and with others. Such an approach will serve to minimize the impact of any of your weaknesses.

It should also be your goal to seek transparency from others.

Acknowledge Your Strengths and Interests

If you are good at doing something or are passionate about pursuing something (interested enough to do it on your own time), letting those in authority (your boss included) know this information can help them look for opportunities for you to pursue your goals. Follow this path with care and subtlety, however, as appearing to be pushy and a suck-up will likely count against you with your boss and your colleagues. Remember to respect the skills of your colleagues who may be experts in the areas where you are weak, and don't try to get in the way of them doing their jobs; possibly offer to assist them as a means of gaining experience.

Don't try to be a master of everything—it simply isn't possible. Instead, try to be a master of a few things and generally good and skilled in other relevant areas. Don't be a "Jack of all trades and master of none," as this superficiality will be a career limiter. The more rounded your skills are, the better you will be in balancing priorities as you progress into management.

A Psychological Perspective

In psychology, one personality trait scale is called "options" and "procedures." A person with extreme "procedures" tendencies will always stick to the tried and tested methods they have used in the past, even if they a not appropriate: "To a person with only a hammer, everything looks like a nail." A person with extreme "options" tendencies will look at everything as an opportunity to try something new and test new ideas—a tendency that is common among technology staff with an interest in learning different skills. Unfortunately, in doing so, they never get to the point of learning from their mistakes, and quality delivery suffers as they flit from idea to idea: "We learn by doing." "Options" personality types often fail to deliver and leave others to the day-to-day detail. A good architect needs to be perfectly balanced on this personality trait and know when to stick to what is already in use and when to try something new. Sadly, many architects transition from their role as developers and look continually for new technology toys to fill their workday; they will never be good architects.

You need to be working hard and doing a good job with your current responsibilities before executives are likely to want to unleash you into new areas. Until they see competency and ideally mastery in what you currently are responsible for, they will not want to incur the risks of giving you more responsibilities.

Managers are not mind readers, and they will not know to be on the lookout for opportunities for you if you don't inform them of your strengths and interests. But don't come forward with every new hot technology as the latest and greatest interest area. Bring forward only those ideas that you are truly passionate about, not what looks to be an attempt to stuff your resume or a display of flashy object syndrome (the inability to focus on what you are currently doing, in favor of focusing on whatever looks flashy, new, and trendy).

Beat the Crowd to Your Boss

One of the first things you will learn as an architect is that there is a well-worn path from many different parts of the organization to your boss's office. All of the people who make this pilgrimage have their normal items that they need to talk about, but they will also likely comment on how you interact with their organization and what effects, positive or negative, you have on them.

Knowing the reality of how information is socialized through your organization will make you more cautious in what you say and do. For your own benefit, you are far better off sprinting to your boss's office in person to let him or her know what you said or did (your latest transgression) rather than allowing the organizational network to craft its message and deliver it to your boss.

Remember, bosses and executives should receive no surprises. Telling your boss about your latest issue or an event that could be perceived as a transgression gives your boss time to prepare to defend you—even though you might initially be given a dressing-down—rather than having to hastily come to your rescue when something unexpected is raised. Forcing your boss to put out a fire in this way certainly won't help your career progression.

If the organization has an opportunity to communicate the information to your boss before you get to his office, two things will happen. First, your boss will have had no context about what happened and will be put in a spot where he has to respond to raw information and must assume that it is mostly or at least partially correct. Second, he will be irritated that you have not disclosed something to him in a timely manner. This omission will erode trust, which is a valuable commodity. You can let the grapevine provide news about you to your boss a few times, but don't make it a habit.

In contrast, if you make it to your boss first, she can hear the story first-hand. When you share this information, you need to be upfront about what you did; don't color the story to your benefit because the truth will be disclosed shortly anyway. This does several things for your boss:

- It demonstrates that you are trustworthy even when the going gets tough. However, if you don't provide full disclosure, you may be digging yourself a deeper hole.
- It allows your boss to prepare for the onslaught of those people who are likely to be queuing up in the hallway and allows her to have a reasonable response to what she is about to hear. People don't always feel comfortable dealing with conflict directly. Instead, they may choose to deal with your superior. By having disclosed the item first, you change the dynamics of the conversation the person and your boss will have. The reporter suddenly appears to be the one with a problem—he may even be seen as a tattletale for not having dealt directly with you about the issue, and then raising the issue higher only if the issue was not resolved.
- It allows the organization to know that you have a good working relationship with your boss, and managers may not feel as inclined to meddle in the problem because they know that it will be handled effectively without their involvement.

PROJECT TRANSPARENCY

The second kind of transparency is project transparency. It includes areas such as letting executives see all of the good points and the bad points within a project (full information will help them help you to be successful), exposing risks, opportunities for cost savings, and assumptions. The goal is to make the key elements of a project plainly visible to all.

Let Executives See All the Cards

With major projects or initiatives, an astounding number of details must be recognized and managed effectively. Some of them are easy to identify and deal with. Others are more subtle and require executive help to work through.

When you are dealing with executives, it best to put all the cards on the table face up: Executives are good at this game and can help make the best of a potentially bad situation (see Figure 6-2). Hiding things because you think you can "manage it" without their knowledge will come back and haunt you later.

Figure 6-2   Let executives see all of your cards.

The notion of transparency needs to be in full force when you are interacting with executives. Their ability and interest level in helping work through critical moments of a project will be directly correlated to your prior behavior with respect to disclosure.

As a project is first conceptualized, moves on to seeking approval, and finally begins its journey with full or partial funding, the executives involved both directly and indirectly with the project need to be aware of what is going on. They are motivated to ensure that the company's revenue numbers are met and expenses are held to a minimum.

When you fully disclose to them what is happening (literally the good, the bad, and the ugly), they can advise you on the best course of action to take and can step in and help deal with higher-level organizational negotiations when necessary. Of course, executives are busy people, so when points of executive interest are raised, they should be summarized succinctly, neutrally, and directly with no "technobabble." Give a technology-based summary only when asked to do so by the executives. Your willingness to see things from their point of view and accommodate that perspective in your executive briefing will be appreciated.

Executive involvement at the right time can greatly smooth the way during the execution of projects. However, if you have failed to be open or to recognize the flashing yellow lights along the way indicating danger ahead, the executives' ability to do something to help the project may be severely handicapped. If the situation is bad enough, they will work to ensure that you don't get the opportunity to put them in that situation again.

When issues must be dealt with, take the time to work through at least three viable alternatives for their resolution and have a recommended approach for executives to approve or disapprove. Most importantly, when presenting the issue, the options, and the recommended solution, be succinct and stick to the facts.

Architects Bring Transparency and Clarity to Many Areas

Architects need to live in the world of what is possible. As the company seeks to make investments in particular areas, architects help bring transparency and clarity about the risks, possible approaches, and key assumptions for each project entailed in transforming the vision into reality.

Architects can help determine the level of investment that will be needed. The business (new product development, marketing, and sales) can determine the possible business value in making the investment. The combination of the two can help determine the all-important return on investment (ROI).

The architect is both part of the business and responsible to it. Fulfilling those roles requires ensuring that there is some value in everything that is used and delivered. Meeting this standard may mean you don't get the best hardware or system software due to cost concerns, but such compromises must be accepted.

The architect needs to understand the business needs and transparently react to them rather than seeking to work around them. Nevertheless, you should keep in mind that future agility or interoperability also has value in itself that is often more difficult to quantify. Thus, if your desired approach helps in this area, and if the business is active in the arena of mergers and acquisitions, this consideration poses a valid challenge to the business's basic tenet of assessing value based on ROI.

If you are using legacy systems, the software debt or design debt may require more investment at a minimum level to avoid problems with support or change later on. This is another area to discuss clearly and concisely with the business representatives. Garnering adequate funding in such a case will likely require you to be a salesman for your part of the business.

For many companies, the value for a particular project can literally range from a negative ROI to many multiples of the investment. Typically, many other factors determine what this value should be: Is the project considered strategic (a lower value may be acceptable), or is it considered more tactical (a higher value may be required)?

Architects Bring Discovery to Acquisition

Discovery is the need to foster transparency in an acquisition project for a company that is about to be purchased. The owners of the target company have a clear incentive to get the most dollars for their assets and their brand, so they may not want to fully disclose all of the details related to the firm's problematic issues or, if they do make this information available, they may want to spin it in a slightly more positive light. As an architect involved in due diligence work, your goal is to bring transparency to the assets that are about to be purchased (see Figure 6-3).

Often, the enterprise and infrastructure architects are responsible for appraising the value of an asset to the business in a merger, takeover, or acquisition in terms of cost, depreciation, replacement value, integration value, business return on investment, and even removal costs. In this role,

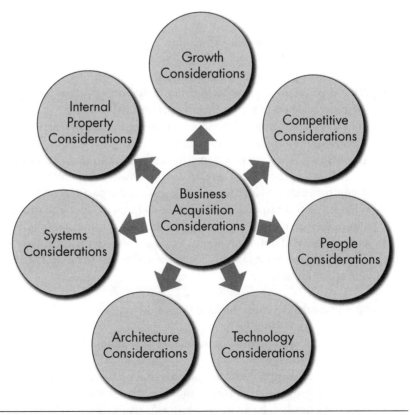

Figure 6-3 Company acquisitions need to consider many different, but related, vectors of information.

the architect is a key part of the business team in valuing the business itself and planning for the future.

In an acquisitions situation, key business considerations include the following:

- Which elements of the company are providing the value? Why do you want to purchase the firm? Because of the people? Because of the processes? Because of the technology? Because of the domain knowledge?
- How might you potentially goof up this company and its strategy?
- Which liabilities will your company assume as a result of this acquisition?
- Is the company an established market leader?
- What is your company's strategy?
- Is there overlap with what you currently do?
- Is this a good fit?

Key growth considerations include the following:

- What is the opportunity for growth?
- What if you want to grow by 10 times or 100 times—can the target company scale up to match those expectations?
- Does the target company possess knowledge about a particular market that your company wants to enter?
- Are there areas of your company that are weak and that the partner can help strengthen? Are there areas where your company brings strength and can fill an area of weakness for the partner?
- What if you want to take what the target company does and move it into the international market—can the partner internationalize its operations? If not, what are the costs for remedying these issues? Can any shortcomings in this be overcome, or has the firm taken its concept as far as it can go?

Key competitive considerations include the following:

- Are other key competitors in the marketplace about to overtake the partner's advantages?
- Do other key competitors have patents that may prevent your company from growing the business into the areas it wants to enter?
- How hard would it be for a competitor to replicate what the target company has done?

Key people considerations include the following:

- Who are the key technology leaders?
- Are any members of your company's due diligence or purchasing approval team friends or strong acquaintances with the selling company's employees or board of directors?
- Who are the key staff—particularly architects—who understand how the whole environment fits together?

Key technology considerations include the following:

- What are the technologies being used?
- How well is the technology constructed?
- Do you understand the company's technology well enough to model it? If you don't, have you investigated enough?

Key architecture considerations include the following:

- Where is the target company on the technology adoption stack?
- Is it using technologies that are obsolete or about to become obsolete?
- Is its technology architecture compatible with your company's architecture?
- How close is the partner's technology stack to your own company's technology stack? And how well might they potentially mesh together?
- Which industry standards does the partner follow? Are they the same as your company's standards, or is everything proprietary?
- Does the target company suffer from software debt, design debt, depreciation, or just poor support and strategy?
- Do you understand its domain well enough? If you don't, have you investigated enough?

Key systems considerations include the following:

- Which integration, messaging, and service bus technologies does the partner have that can be leveraged?
- Can the target company's key business services and processes be accessed behind a controlled interface to avoid tight coupling dependencies?
- Which key systems are required to run the partner's business that overlap with the ones your company already has?

- Is the partner's support of its key services adequate to facilitate integration?
- Are its processes, systems, and infrastructure documented?
- Are some of its systems long lacking for support?

Key intellectual property considerations include the following:

- Does the partner have inventory management for licenses, hardware, software, and other assets?
- Are there currently key licensing agreements in place that enable the target company to do its business?
- How does the partner use open-source materials? Is it complying with the nature of the licensing agreements?
- Are there intellectual property constraints surrounding the technologies? Are there patents? Are there trademarks? Are there key trade secrets? Does any type of intellectual property protection give the target company a competitive advantage and allow it to continue to hold or improve its current positioning in the marketplace? Does the firm license any of this intellectual property to other companies?

All of these considerations speak to clarity:

- **Clarity of vision.** Where do you want to go?
- **Clarity of weakness.** What will prevent you from achieving your goal?
- **Clarity of assumptions.** What do you fundamentally believe to be true? What are risks are you incurring by making these assumptions?
- **Clarity of operating models.** How does this company work?
- **Clarity of opportunity.** What can be leveraged from both companies? What are areas of duplication or redundancy (and can they easily be eliminated)? Which costs can be removed? Will any divestitures be required by government agencies?

The answers to these questions will help you determine the current value and potential future value of the proposed acquisition.

Many questions need answering when a merger or acquisition is contemplated, but the architect knows what to ask, how to understand the responses and follow up, and how to draw and document the information as it relates to all levels of the existing business. For integration in any kind of merger or acquisition, the architect is a critical business resource whose value to the organization (and promotion prospects) increases as more merger activity is undertaken. When due diligence investigations are ongoing, professionalism and transparency of operations are needed on both sides—that is, from the company doing the acquiring as well as form the company being acquired. Nevertheless, care must be taken to ensure that this disclosure does not come at the expense of revealing trade secrets until the merger is finalized. To perform this work effectively, the architect must understand the business strategy of his or her own company.

RELATIONAL TRANSPARENCY

The third kind of transparency is relational transparency. It deals with transparency with respect to others. This area includes such considerations as giving credit to others; consistently giving everyone the same message; apologizing to others; listening to others, so that you can hear before you react; and allowing others to be transparent with you. Again, the goal with transparency is to enhance trust.

Give Credit to Others Where Credit Is Due

Throughout the organization, sparks of insight may be seen about how to solve a particular problem, how to model something, how to scale something—the list goes on and on. As you are interacting with others, share the names of those who helped bring this concept into reality, who designed a particular solution, or who jumped on the fumble.

This gracious approach to giving credit serves many purposes. In particular, it allows you to fan the spark provided by the individual into a flame, thereby bringing broader recognition (and a potential promotion) to someone who clearly deserves to receive a few accolades. It will help others gain confidence in knowing they can make real contributions to the company's success, and suggest to them that they should consider taking on more responsibility and growing in their careers.

Giving credit also shows to others that you are a person of integrity; you could have easily claimed responsibility without anyone's knowledge to the contrary, but you chose to allow the spotlight to shine on someone. At the end of the day, you can feel good about what you did and how you are helping others in the organization grow into their potential.

Later, when you encounter other challenging problems, your colleagues will likely be more than happy to help you out, knowing that you will work with their best interests at heart and that you will give them opportunities to show those higher up in the organization (executives to whom they may not have regular access) which capabilities they possess.

When you are in trouble and in need of assistance, if you have given credit to all those deserving of it, they will most likely rally round to stop a minor problem becoming a disaster for you. As you can see, having a large group of friends to call on in an emergency is in your own interest.

When promotions come around, the ability to sell a promotion for someone else is much easier if those in the management chain have heard a regular cadence of good things a particular employee has done versus a one-time sales pitch that on the surface looks to be a bit overstated. Executives also look with favor on those who have shown grace to their colleagues, considering them to be "team players" whose own careers are worthy of being furthered.

Be Consistent in What You Say

As a leader in the organization, you need to be careful not only in what you say, but in how you say it and in the consistency with which you say it. The words you say, the words you type in email, the presentations you prepare, and the documents you produce should all be consistent. The message you are trying to convey needs to be repeated, but not altered in its core direction based on audience.

Architects have a relatively high technical profile with a company. Consequently, the words they say tend to be repeated throughout the organization—so think about what you say. Sometimes the best course may be to avoid the flippant comment or funny remark you are dying to make, lest it be misinterpreted.

If what you say to different parts of the organization is not consistent—whether your intention is to avoid conflict or to try to sell something—you are introducing issues that you will need to deal with in the future. If the areas that receive the different "messages" meet and share their experience, the only casualty will be any trust they have for you—so be warned.

Deal with the conflict up front and give people a chance to hear both sides of an issue. Most people will try to do the right thing with respect to what is best for the company, even when it may affect their own positions negatively.

Apologizing Demonstrates Transparency

There really is no truer sense of transparency than when you apologize to others and mean what you are saying. Rendering a heartfelt apology helps to reestablish trust for a relationship with the other person.

It is never too early or too late to apologize. If something happened recently and it is nagging you, swallow your pride and apologize; both you and the other person will feel better about the situation. If you have waited a long time and the situation is still nagging you, even though the other person has probably long since forgotten the incident, take the time and apologize. Your pride will not be permanently damaged, and the apology will allow your mind to focus in on other things.

Learn to Hear Before You React (Seek Transparency)

Have you ever been listening to a conversation and just itching for the other person to end his or her speech so you can get in that brilliant point or show that you have already solved a problem that may not exist?

This is not transparency.

In such a case, you are neither seeking transparency (the real thing that the other person is telling you or, more subtly, not directly saying) nor being transparent yourself. In fact, the only thing you are revealing about yourself is that you really don't care about the conversation, but instead care more about yourself.

You need to learn to listen and hear before you react—an approach that will help establish trust (see Figure 6-4). Wait and hold your comments; there is likely no imminent doom that will occur if you wait just a few minutes to fully hear what the other person has to say.

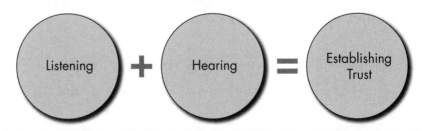

Figure 6-4 Listening to and hearing what a person is saying helps establish trust.

You may be worried you won't score points if you don't make your comment—but scoring points, of course, is just bad behavior. More likely, you are worried you will forget your point. If so, mentally note the key phrases and go back to listening; as you may find, the speaker has already anticipated your perceived issue and addressed it. Save yourself the embarrassment of jumping in with both feet too soon: Wait, listen, and understand what is being said. Integrate the message into your own mental framework representation of the problem domain and test your understanding before responding.

Allow Others to Be Transparent with You

By modeling transparency in your actions, you allow others to be less defensive and more open in their interactions with you. Transparency is all about building trust in all working relationships. It offers many benefits:

- The teams with which you interact will be more comfortable working with you because you have built up trust. They can then happily reach out and ask for help early on when an issue is small and first discovered. Capturing this kind of information early on will allow you to lend a helping hand and deal with an issue before it has a chance to grow into a major ordeal.
- The teams with which you interact will be more likely to bring challenges, concerns, and issues directly to you versus raising them up the team's management chain and then managing them down your own management chain.
- When the next project rolls around, the teams will likely request that you be on the team, because they know that you will work toward ensuring the success of the entire team.
- Maintaining transparency allows you to coach the teams to be able to make better decisions on their own. When you are not around, the teams will still understand the principles and domain knowledge that you use to drive your decision-making process.

Allowing others to be transparent toward you will serve both you and the project's work, thereby improving the chances of success.

BECOMING A TRANSPARENT ARCHITECT

The road to becoming transparent begins with the following steps:

- Realizing that architects live in a glass house.
- Self-transparency:
  - Be yourself.

- Acknowledge your weaknesses.
- Acknowledge your strengths and interests.
- Beat the crowd to your boss.
- Project transparency:
  - Let executives see all the cards.
  - Realize that architects can bring transparency and clarity to many areas.
  - Bring discovery to business acquisition.
- Relational transparency:
  - Give credit to others where credit is due.
  - Be consistent in what you say.
  - Learn to apologize.
  - Learn to hear before you react.
  - Allow others to be transparent with you.

Becoming an architect who embraces transparency leads you down a road filled with success. The biggest hurdle to overcome is your own pride. The good news is that most people are more than willing to accept the real you and will appreciate your openness.

BIBLIOGRAPHY

Bassett, Lucinda. (2001). *Life Without Limits.* Cliff Street Books.

Covey, Stephan R. (2000). *Principle Centered Leadership.* Simon & Schuster.

Covey, Stephan R. (2008). *The Speed of Trust: The One Thing That Changes Everything* [Audio CD]. Simon & Schuster Audio.

Goldsmith, Marshall. (2007). *What Got You Here Won't Get You There: How Successful People Become Even More Successful* [Audio CD]. Random House Audio.

Maxwell, John C. (1998). *The 21 Irrefutable Laws of Leadership: Follow Them and People Will Follow.* Thomas Nelson.

Montoya, Peter; Vandehev, Tim. (2005). *The Brand Called You: The Ultimate Personal Branding Handbook to Transform Anyone into an Indispensible Brand.* Peter Montoya Publishing.

Patterson, Kerry; Grenny, Joseph; McMillan, Ron; Switzler, Al. (2002). *Crucial Conversations: Tools for Talking When Stakes Are High.* McGraw-Hill.

Chapter 7

PASSION

Passion, it lies in all of us, sleeping . . . waiting . . . and though unwanted . . . unbidden . . . it will stir . . . open its jaws and howl. It speaks to us . . . guides us . . . passion rules us all, and we obey. What other choice do we have? Passion is the source of our finest moments. The joy of love . . . the clarity of hatred . . . and the ecstasy of grief. It hurts sometimes more than we can bear. If we could live without passion maybe we'd know some kind of peace . . . but we would be hollow . . . Empty rooms shuttered and dank. Without passion we'd be truly dead.

—Joss Whedon, American Screenwriter[1]

Nothing great in the world has been accomplished without passion.

—Georg Wilhelm Friedrich Hegel, German Philosopher and Inventor

Passion is the genesis of genius.

—Anthony Robbins, American Advisor to Leaders

If you have worked in a business environment for more than a couple of years, you may begin to feel overwhelmed by the resistance of the organization that allows it to stay unchanged, and by the glacial pace at which things sometimes move. Perhaps you have amazing ideas for all kinds of things, but getting those ideas through the gauntlet of the product business cycle to actually reach a customer can begin to wear you down.

As time progresses, that small voice (your passion, the source of the ideas) begins to quiet. The excitement you first had gives way to a slower, less exciting and more realistic cadence. You may even feel as if the weight of the organization has literally bound you up, making it hard to breath.

---

1. Joss Whedon. Great-Quotes.com, Gledhill Enterprises, 2011. Retrieved June 14, 2011, from http://www.great-quotes.com/quote/40898

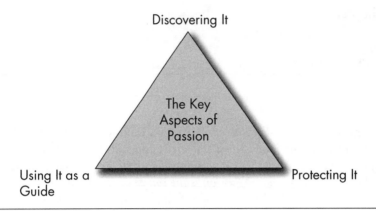

Figure 7-1   Passion is the internal fire that can propel your career.

After the initial flame of enthusiasm is quenched, it is hard to get your passion rekindled. You need to recognize the warning signs that the flame is dimming and learn to adjust your environment to allow you to pursue a meaningful life and career. If you feel your flame has been put out completely and your role is no longer enjoyable, now is the time to move on to another company to rekindle the passion you once had, rather than simply settling for a miserable job where you never strive to "do better."

This chapter shows you how to find, use, protect, and actively pursue passion as a key soft skill that will enable you to find success as a software architect (see Figure 7-1).

WHAT IS PASSION?

Passion (from the Latin verb *patior*, meaning "to suffer" or "to endure") is a very strong feeling about a person or thing. Passion is an intense feeling, enthusiasm, or desire for something. It can be expressed as a feeling of unusual excitement, enthusiasm, or compelling emotion toward a subject, idea, person, or object. A person is said to have a passion for something when he has a strong positive affinity for it.[2]

For me, passion revolves around those things that I would be naturally inclined to want to do or to think about in my free time. No one has to

---

2. "Passion." *Wikipedia*. (2011). Wikimedia Foundation, Inc. October 9, 2010.
   http://en.wikipedia.org/wiki/Passion_(emotion)

ask me to do it. No one has to pay me to do it. It just naturally consumes my thoughts. The key is to begin applying action toward those thoughts. Obviously, we are referring here to the business context and your role as an architect; any other passion wouldn't be appropriate in the workplace. As you slowly gain expertise in a particular area, your interests and fascination with that particular area can grow and provide you with new opportunities—opportunities that can help you enjoy what you do every day.

Work surrounded by passion feels less like an obligation and more like a great day to do what you love to do.

DISCOVERING PASSION

One of the best things you can do to help your career is discover the things that you are passionate about.

How Do I Find Passion?

The people you work with know what you are passionate about. When you talk to them, certain topics and activities cause your eyes to light up, your voice to be enthusiastic, your body posture to be engaged—you don't need to tell anyone, because your whole body will shout the message. The reverse is also true: If you truly lack passion about something, there is almost nothing you can do to overcome your body shouting, "Please, just put me out of my misery now!"

Listen to what you say to others, and how you say it, when you are consumed by the conversation and the rest of the world fades away.

Learn about body language and study the way other people present themselves and their ideas to figure out what they really feel about a subject—and then apply the same techniques to look at the way you present yourself. If your body language contradicts what your lips are saying about your passion for a subject, look for some nuance to pique your interest when communicating with others. Make yourself passionate about your work and the quality of your work, but recognize that there are always some things we are more interested in than others; that is, we have a natural desire to spend more time on some things than others.

What is that small voice saying? It may not speak loudly, but listen to it once in a while; it is usually a dream that is trying to get out. Let it out—don't bury it in the endless set of activities that are clamoring for your attention. These are areas you are likely to be passionate about.

Find some quiet time to sit down and write out your interests (see Figure 7-2). This exercise may start out slowly. The ideas may seem odd or goofy at first, but write them down anyway. As more ideas start coming, keep writing everything down—there are no wrong answers.

Let a few weeks or months pass. Try the exercise again. Do you see repeated patterns when you compare the lists? Have some things already happened? (Don't be too surprised—things have usually already started to manifest themselves.)

I usually keep the list of these things in my wallet; they are always with me. Some of the items may never become reality, but at least I am aware of them. Over time—sometimes years later—I forget what was on an earlier list, and I find that I have addressed many of the items and new opportunities have managed to present themselves in ways not quite as I imagined. Nonetheless, the outcomes are clearly related to some of the earlier thoughts that were merely seeds.

Identification of your passions gives you additional information when you are weighing options in making a particular decision and gives you a better understanding which path to take. At least for me, the answers are not always clear.

My final decision usually comes at the last moment, after I have had time to write down the pros and cons related to a decision (usually from both sides—if I choose one path, what are the pros and cons; if I choose a different path, what are the pros and cons—and then compare the options). For some reason, it is not until the last minute that clarity presents itself.

By consciously capturing areas that you are passionate about (and these areas are likely to change over time) and by being willing to take some

Figure 7-2   Keep a list of the things that grab your attention—wishes, dreams, things that seem interesting or fun. These are the seeds of your passion.

risks to pursue the things that inspire your passion, you may find that your dreams are probably just around the corner. Even if they aren't, or even if the destination isn't quite what you expected, you may still enjoy the journey.

Persistence and Passion: The Ultimate Killer Combination

Mastery of a particular area usually comes only with dogged persistence. It seems like there are 10,000 ways to do things wrong and only a handful of ways to do them right. For me, mastery usually requires running at a problem repeatedly, making mistakes, learning, running at the problem again, and repeating the process again. Each time I learn from the previous iteration and try something slightly different or take a different approach.

Each time I approach the problem from a different angle, I try to step back and think, and perhaps study the area by examining documentation or books to see what I was doing wrong. Usually, however, I end up giving it another try.

After a while, the nuances of the real problem I am trying to solve emerge, and I finally start to understand what needs to be done and why it needs to be done a particular way. The next time I am faced with a similar problem, I can reuse all of the knowledge that I so painfully gained to shorten the amount of time to solve the current problem.

On the surface, someone who has mastered a particular area makes it look easy. If you talk to the person, however, you usually find the individual traveled a long and winding road to gain the knowledge and experience she now possesses.

For me, it usually is not until I have resolved in my heart, "No matter what, I am going to pursue this problem until it gets resolved," that the solution begins to emerge from the faint details of each new piece of information discovered. Each piece of the puzzle reveals itself only when diligently pursued.

The areas you are passionate about require the same kind of tenacity. You must be willing to deal with setbacks, course adjustments, and putting in the extra effort to bring what you are passionate about to life. It seems as if challenges are the universe's way of asking you, "Do you really, really want this?" Until you are willing to answer, "Yes, I am committed—not just today, but for the long haul," the universe will keep asking the same question.

By combining persistence and passion, you will create the ultimate killer combination: something you love to do and the strength and endurance to keep on going even when obstacles are put into your path. This is how dreams live and die. It is also how we learn—by making mistakes and picking ourselves up to try again.

Passion over Position

Occasionally, the desire to advance in the company for which you work may overwhelm your thinking, so that you consider taking positions that are not in areas that you truly care about. Perhaps the position looks great from a monetary perspective and an increased responsibility perspective, but fails to capture your heart. In these situations, consider the long-term effects of taking the position. If you are not able to advance beyond this next position:

- Can you enjoy the work required of this position?
- Can you enjoy working with the people associated with this position?
- Can you enjoy solving the types of problems this position is responsible for?
- Can you work in the political environment the position brings?
- Can your family survive the extra time commitments needed?
- Does this position align with your long-term goals?

If the answer to any of these questions is no, you need to seriously consider what will happen when the honeymoon period of getting this position wears off and the daily grind sets in. Can you find something that makes you want to get up in the morning to do the required work (and no, making more money is not the answer)? If you lose your passion for doing the work, your ability to produce excellent work will diminish. Your boss and those around you may question whether you are the right person for the position. Even if you never get to the point where you job is jeopardized, do you really want to spend your valuable life doing something that fails to inspire you?

If the answer to most of the preceding questions is yes, you should seriously consider applying for the position. Change is a good thing. It gives you the opportunity to learn new things, find out different ways to solve new problems, expand your network of relationships, and grow as an individual. Even if this position is more of a lateral move, it will show those above you in the organizational hierarchy that you are capable of handling a broad set of problems and are resilient to change. This is a great message to share, because businesses are constantly changing and they need to know that as new and more challenging business problems arise, you are up to the task of slaying the new dragons.

Rekindling Passion

Occasionally, life loses its sense of excitement and a sense of a dull routine seems to engulf you—you can feel it, you can sense it. In this environment, the enthusiasm to do much of anything seems to be absent. If you sense this lassitude coming on or you are already bogged down in ennui, it's time to take a break, regroup, and consider which ideas might energize you.

Sometimes, just getting away for a few days can help clear your head. For example, I usually take every Friday off during the summer. These three-day weekends at the lake allow me to unwind from everything that has happened over the course of the week. As the summer progresses, I can feel myself being rejuvenated, and the things that were beginning to bore me start to take on new life. It's like a breeze fanning the flame. My outlook brightens and I am ready to take on a whole new set of problems with vigor and enthusiasm.

The Value of Exercise

Another strategy that can dramatically improve your outlook is to get out and exercise, even if it's just walking for a couple of miles in the morning or evening. If you can't do this, park a few blocks from work or take the stairs. It's amazing how just a little activity can have a dramatic impact on your perception of what is happening around you and your ability to be more accommodating (and less irritated) by life's daily hassles. The higher the level of stress associated with your position, the more activity you may want to pursue. Exercise will truly help keep you healthy, wealthy, and wise.

If a vacation isn't possible, exercise produces endorphins that can stimulate and relax the body, thereby producing a positive attitude. All it takes is just a little change to help rekindle the spark.

USING PASSION AS A GUIDE

Let your passion help guide you to the right path (see Figure 7-3). Passion can be used as a force in helping you decide

- Which things you should pursue
- Which things you should ignore

You   Passion

Figure 7-3 Let passion help you decide which roads to follow.

Watch for Opportunity: It Usually Seeks You and Speaks Quietly

It is an odd paradox, but the best route to goals (at least for me) is not always a straight-line, forward path. Most of the areas that, when I look back, have turned into areas of success for me were not things I was directly pursuing. It seems that whenever life gets noisy and the number of distractions is running high, opportunity seems to present itself off to the side, not with a lot of fanfare, but speaking in a faint voice that compels me to listen closely. When I can unravel myself from the commotion surrounding me and not be caught up in the brew-ha-ha, I can begin to hear the voice of opportunity—the chance to pursue what I am passionate about. This opportunity is usually not packaged in the manner that I had imagined, but it still presents the essence of what I am fascinated in pursuing. The challenge for me is to listen diligently enough to hear and internalize what is being said, and not to be drawn away by the loud distractions.

This situation has arisen in relation to many of the job opportunities I have had over my career—I have had my mind clearly set on one path when a unique opportunity presented itself. Such an opportunity can come from an unexpected direction and at a time when I least expect it. The first challenge is to see the opportunity, given the current momentum and focus on what is directly in front of me. At first, the change seems like a 90° hard left, at least until I begin slowing down and contemplating the essence of what has presented itself.

Think about such an opportunity this way: The situation is analogous to speeding down the highway and seeing some glimmer out of the corner of your eye. At first, you are not quite sure what it is, but you have a gut feeling that is important. Do I keep on truckin' down the highway (I have deadlines to keep and plans formulated) or do I take the time to slow down, turn around, and find out more about the glimmer off to the side that I just missed? When I have the presence of mind to disengage for just a moment and fully consider the opportunity, I have rarely been disappointed in pursuing it.

If you enthusiastically engage with everyone you work with—from colleagues, to managers, to customers, to vendors—and show tenacity and skill in everything you do, opportunity can be around every corner. Often, those you engage with will be the source of these events. Customers and vendors may bring opportunities to learn and excel, so don't neglect them; your willingness to embrace such opportunities will reflect back on the company.

Follow Your Instincts

In today's media-centric world, trying to find and hear your inner voice (your instincts) can be challenging. When you first start to estimate projects, try guessing first. You may be surprised to find that, after you have done your top-down analysis and your bottom-up analysis, your initial guess (read gut feel, instinct) was in the ball park. If it's not, learn a little, and try again the next time. Often, rough project sizing requests come up with extremely small time frames (sometimes less than 30 minutes). You need to learn how to build some form of a model from which you can begin viewing the problem from multiple perspectives. This mechanism will help validate that your "guess" is somewhat reasonable.

If you get in a situation where things just don't feel right, and you can't quite explain why, back out. Your instincts should guide you. After a while, you will notice a sixth sense about situations—either you are at peace with what is happening or you sense something is wrong. Listen to this sixth sense; it can guide you out of troublesome areas when you don't know all of the details.

When you get ideas in your head, write them down. Ponder alternatives and other details about the ideas. The idea may be a great new design or an approach, so take the time to capture it. The still, small voices that inject ideas into your thinking can often produce the breakthroughs that you need to solve a particular problem.

There is a scientific basis to this process—that is, the way your instincts highlight things to you. The human brain consists of two hemispheres, with the left brain doing slow and thorough conscious analysis and the right brain doing the creativity and looking at "the big picture."[3] The conscious

---

3. http://viewzone2.com/bicamx.html

thought you put into your work in IT is primarily the work of the left brain, whereas the subconscious and the right brain are looking out for you at a more expansive level. The little voice? It's your subconscious telling you that it has done the "big picture" work and spotted a problem—it just doesn't have the detailed communication skills of the left brain that would enable it to explain the idea directly to you. That's why we solve so many problems in our sleep and wake up with ideas for solving problems. Learn to listen to your subconscious!

Choose Areas That You Are Passionate About

When opportunity knocks, try to keep the financial considerations at bay for at least some period of time. Think about the pros and cons of each opportunity from the perspectives of "if you take it" and "if you don't": What are the impacts? Think about how the opportunity will affect both you and your family. Think about how well it aligns with the areas that excite you and cause you to melt away in your thinking.

Recognize that you, like every other human being, have different motivators. According to Abraham Maslow's hierarchy of needs, people have a series of needs (read: motivators) that are organized into a pyramid, where needs must be fulfilled from the bottom of the pyramid upward. At the bottom level are physiological needs such as the need for food and water; they are built upon by safety needs such as a home, health, and employment, along with love needs such as a family. Money at its most fundamental is associated with these levels, because it enables us to live securely. The upper levels of Maslow's hierarchy consist of esteem, where we look for respect from others and self-respect, and self-actualization, such as occurs through creativity and problem solving.

Within the hierarchy of needs, we seek first to fulfill our needs at the bottom of the hierarchy and then move farther up the pyramid. Thus, once we have enough money to be secure in the first three levels of the pyramid, our motivators become self-respect, which we may achieve through the way we behave honestly and professionally, and respect from others, which we may get from our status in management or from our colleagues through our interactions and professionalism.

When evaluating any proposed new role, consider your passions and determine whether the top level of the pyramid would still apply to you: Would you still be able to express your creativity and solve problems in your own unique way? If not, then the job probably isn't for you unless you yearn to adapt to solving different types of problems and creatively handling new challenges that are different from those you face today.

Pick the path that you will love, and the money will follow. If it doesn't, at least you will enjoy the journey you are on.

Change: The Kick in the Pants to Get You Moving Again

If you have finally reached the point where that once sparkling and exciting career has turned into drudgery, and it seems like going to work will continue to suck the life out of you until you evaporate, you seriously need to consider change. Don't run out and quit your job; unless you are independently wealthy, you probably need the cash flow to keep yourself financially afloat.

Think about what excites you today, what makes you happy, what gives you a sense of fulfillment. If you don't know, consider helping out someone else. It might seem odd, but sometimes helping others find or achieve what they are looking for can help you rediscover what you were looking for. Even if you don't find it right away, your sense of self-worth and general outlook on life will improve dramatically when you help others.

Consider learning a new skill or technology that could be applied at work to bring some sense of change into your current role. At one extreme, contribute to books, magazines, standards bodies, and the general industry community as a way of bringing change to your current role by changing yourself; this effort will bring increased self-esteem along with the more tangible results.

Once you fan the embers of your daily living, you may begin to see ways to change and opportunities that you can begin pursuing on a small scale. Try to figure out if the new interest is really what you want or which aspect of it you like. If this interest really engages you, look for ways to turn it into more of a full-time pursuit.

Once you have made the change, you will be amazed at the amount of energy it produces and how it reinvigorates your life. Your new pursuits will make you want to smile every day, simply because life is good. You may not be making as much money, but money—although necessary—truly is not everything.

Lack of Passion Acts as a Ceiling to Your Career

In my position as an architect, I get the opportunity to interview people on a regular basis. Over the years, I have had a chance to see some hiring decisions turn out to be amazing and others turn out to be less than stellar. Among the ones that did not turn out so well, a definite pattern cannot always be seen. In contrast, among the ones that have excelled, the pattern is clear.

During the interview, as I look for details about the work the applicant has done in the past, a clear story emerges when the great candidates begin to talk. Not only can they speak to the positions they have had, but they can also recall large volumes of specific details—the kind you would remember if you truly loved solving the problems and spent the time to fully immerse yourself in the nuances of the problem and the solution.

The great candidates typically work on technology even in their spare time. They are fascinated with particular areas and learn everything there is to know about those areas. In many respects, their thirst for knowledge is unquenchable.

This kind of drive and interest in a particular area will get you noticed. Your knowledge and expertise will naturally draw people to you when a particular set of problems crops up. In areas that you are passionate about, your ability to communicate clearly and with authority is demonstrated with the greatest of ease.

The reverse is also true: If you go to work just to punch the clock and get a paycheck, your attitude, approach, and level of knowledge about what you do will be adequate, but it will be clear to everyone around you that you lack any level of passion about your endeavors. When it comes time to finding someone who can get the job done right and on time, the person selected typically will have a passion for attacking the problem. These individuals may include a lackluster employee in the effort, but likely only as a team member, not the leader.

When looking at yourself and when hiring others, what should you look for? Are you seeking lots of skills or experience only? Or is the lack of some small skill worth ignoring if it is offset by a great attitude—by enthusiasm and passion? Enthusiasm and passion are likely to triumph over skills any day, as long as the general skills and background are there to build upon.

Whatever you choose to do, do it with everything you have. Find something about the problem that motivates you, and that will fully engage your heart and soul.

Do the Hard Things Well and Give It Everything You Have

Sometimes you may be asked to do tasks that seem small, unglamorous, and downright hard. The first reaction to this kind of request is typically to contemplate saying no. In your head, you think, "I have better things to do and this certainly was not on my priority list." After a brief amount of time, you reluctantly agree to do what has been asked. Your challenge now is to find the energy to fulfill the request.

The first thing to realize is that someone has asked you to perform the task because the individual trusts that you can solve the problem and get it done. The second thing to realize is that they may be testing you to see whether you can deal with the less desirable tasks and nail them before the higher-profile tasks begin flowing in your direction. Those above you in the organizational hierarchy need to know that you can jump in, take charge, and clean up whatever messes might be lying around. Your successful completion of the task will give them the confidence that you are capable, and not just a dilettante seeking the spotlight. It serves to build up their trust in you—and trust is a valuable commodity. It should also boost your own confidence, by proving that you can take on nearly any task and bring it to completion.

Passion: The Internal Fuel That Supplies Drive

After a while, it seems as if almost any pursuit can lose its sparkle. At first, the drop-off is imperceptible, but over time your energy level slowly dwindles and the enthusiasm you once possessed fades. It is usually at this point in time that you need to dig deep to rediscover what inspired you to begin this pursuit in the first place. Knowing what your passions are and knowing that they may change over time can supply the energy that is needed to keep your momentum moving forward when the environment seems a bit rainy and dreary.

PROTECTING YOUR PASSION

Passion is like a flame. You need to be careful not to let others throw water on it; they will quench it. Learn to protect your passion.

Ignore the Critics: It's Your Passion, Your Vision—Not Theirs

When you are truly passionate about something, that enthusiasm sometimes seems to attract negativity from certain people. Be cautious about sharing your dreams and goals. Not everyone will share your enthusiasm. It is hard to hear people say, "Awww, that's impossible," or "What a silly idea." At this point, your passion is like a fledgling starting out: The dream or idea is not especially strong yet, so it may not take that much to kill it.

If you do choose to share your interest, be prepared to overlook the detractors and realize that it truly is *your* passion, and not theirs—they have their own goals and ideas to pursue. The naysayers may not be actively trying to dissuade you from pursuing your passion; rather, it's just not important to them and they don't share your enthusiasm.

After you have had more time to pursue your goal and you have some success under your belt, it seems like the amount of positive feedback grows naturally. Everyone is drawn to success.

Avoid Distractions

At any given time, there seems to be a never-ending stream of activities that are competing to consume your time. If you are not careful, these activities will sap your time and energy, and result in you losing your focus on what is truly important to you.

Take the time to figure out what your values are and what your priorities are. Write it down. If you don't know where you are trying to go, time will escape you. Even if what you write down is not all that inspiring, simply having some direction is better than having no direction at all. You can improve your vision and change it over time.

Create a "to do" list every day and maintain a list of outstanding tasks to carry over from one day to the next; any additional tasks picked up along the way can then be integrated and prioritized. This helps focus your mind on the tasks linked to your highest priorities, ensuring that you do not lose track of tasks and shove them to the bottom of the pile.

By formalizing what is important to you, you have a better shot at prioritizing what you do each day. This approach allows you to put the blinders on and pursue your passions. You will have a much better sense of which responsibilities you can decline, and which responsibilities (a limited number) you can accept. One of the chief things that you should put aside is the TV. Television has a unique way of devouring time; although it is certainly entertaining and fun to watch the latest programming, it will rob you of the most precious resource you have in pursuing your passions—time.

One of the things I always strive to put high on my priority list is my kids. If they want to play, do something, or buy something, I work to find ways that I can say yes. If they want to buy something, I offer to pay half. If they are willing to put up some of their own money, it must be important; if not, it probably wasn't. If they want to play, unless what I am currently doing is extremely urgent (it rarely truly is), I try to drop what I am doing (or if I can finish it quickly, I do so) and engage with them. After all, they took the time to actually include me in something that is important to them. If you say you will play later, do it; your word is your honor.

Don't procrastinate. If there are tasks you can do now that are higher priority than what you are actually doing (and particularly if what you are doing is staring out of the window wishing for the sun to come out before the weekend), get moving with them now and don't put them off until the last minute. With those tasks safely out of the way, there will be no concerns that they haven't been done; if they take longer than you expected, at least you have completed them and now have time to daydream or do something else. While there are always tasks that need to be done, address the important ones early.

What Is One Thing You Can Do Today to Pursue Your Passion?

Sometimes when you look at the goal you are passionate about pursuing, it can be nearly debilitating just to get started. You see the mountain. You see all of the work it may take. You begin to see the obstacles. Fear creeps in. This is your body telling you to get moving, not in the opposite direction, but toward the goal that consumes your thinking.

Look for one small step that you can take today that will help you get started. Here are a few ideas:

- Is there a book you can read or listen to? (I listen to five or six books each year in my truck on the way to and from work every day; it is only a five-minute drive, but I can still put the time to good use.)
- Is there a class you can take?
- Is there a conference or user group you can attend? Typically, these gatherings have birds-of-a-feather meetings you can attend and meet others with similar interests.

- Is there someone who is already doing what you want to pursue? Could that person act as your mentor?
- Can you join a club or organization in the area where you live that focuses on your interest area?
- Are there blogs written by experts on the Web or tutorial presentations they have written?
- Are there online chat rooms or forums that you can participate in?

Engaging with other people, particularly experts in the field, to bounce ideas off them and learn from them, is a great way to gain experience quickly by learning from others' mistakes. Most experts will happily discuss the wrong turns they took as a warning to others—they learned the hard way, which is why they are experts. If you can't find a local expert, try to find a user group or vendor contact who can introduce you to an expert, even if the contact is only via email.

Write down the things you learn, as a way to accelerate your navigation of the road to "expert." If you know from first principles how things work "under the covers," you always have something to build on. We often learn that following the old medical student adage, "Watch one, do one, teach one," applies just as well to IT. You will learn more by explaining to others what you have learned about your area of passion, and by listening to their questions and trying to answer them. I often hear a little voice in my head saying, "Good question. Why didn't I think of that?" If I can work out the answer, then I have learned something; if not, on my road to being an "expert," I can say, "I'll find out"—and then I have another task to follow up on that aligns with my passion.

The key is to just get moving. The momentum you generate will help refuel your inner commitment and give you the strength to take the next step. After a while, the steps you take become automated—they are now a habit.

LEARN TO JUMP IN AND ENJOY THE RIDE

First you jump off the cliff and you build wings on the way down.

—Ray Bradbury, American Science-Fiction Writer

The only real way to maintain your passion in life is to jump in and, as Nike says, "Just do it." We get enjoyment out of our passion only by engaging in it, not by avoiding it through fear. You need to remember that

Figure 7-4   Sometimes you have to jump without knowing all the details.

- You will never be able to remove all of the obstacles.
- You will never be able to reduce all of the risk.
- You cannot do everything.
- You have to prioritize and choose.
- You have to make the rest of the world vanish, follow your instincts, and jump. Try the small cliffs first.
- Enjoy the journey: Smile on the way down, and if you hit the bottom, get up, dust yourself off, climb back up the hill, and jump off again (see Figure 7-4).

BECOMING A PASSIONATE ARCHITECT

The road to becoming a passionate architect begins with the following steps:

- Understanding what passion is.
- Discovering passion:
    - Understand how to find passion.
    - Combine persistence and passion.
    - Choose passion over position.
    - Rekindling of your passion is occasionally required.
- Using passion as a guide:
    - Watch for the quiet voice of opportunity.
    - Learn to follow your instincts.
    - Choose areas that you are passionate about.
    - Change your environment or circumstance.
    - Realize that a lack of passion will limit your career path.
    - Do the hard things well, and give them everything you have.
    - Supply your drive by using passion as the fuel.

- Protecting passion:
  - Ignore the critics.
  - Avoid distractions.
- Pursuing your passions beginning today.
- Learning to jump in and enjoy the ride.

Becoming an architect who embraces passion means navigating a road filled with excitement, wonder, and a positive outlook. The biggest hurdle to overcome is recognizing when you are going off course and taking corrective action. The good news is that it takes relatively little effort to pursue what you are passionate about, but it does take a bunch of courage.

BIBLIOGRAPHY

Citrin, James M.; Smith, Richard A. (2004). *The 5 Patterns of Extraordinary Careers: The Guide for Achieving Success and Satisfaction.* Crown Business.

Coyle, Daniel. (2009). *The Talent Code: Greatness Isn't Born, It's Grown. Here's How.* Bantam Dell.

Fowler, Chad. (2009). *The Passionate Programmer: Creating a Remarkable Career in Software Development.* Pragmatic Life.

Goleman, Daniel. (2001). *Emotional Intelligence: Why It Can Matter More Than IQ* [Audio CD]. Macmillan Audio.

Maxwell, John C. (2000). *Fail Forward: Turning Mistakes into Stepping Stones for Success.* Thomas Nelson.

Schmitt, Bernd H. (2008). *Big Think Strategy: How to Leverage Bold Ideas and Leave Small Thinking Behind (Your Coach in a Box)* [Audio CD]. Your Coach Digital.

Ziglar, Zig (1994). *Over the Top: Moving from Survival to Stability, from Stability to Success, from Success to Significance.* Thomas Nelson.

Chapter 8

CONTEXT SWITCHING

To do two things at once is to do neither.

—Publilius Syrus, Freed Roman Slave

The role of architect is one that is fundamentally based on fast-paced context switching in an environment that deals with a broad portion of the organization, both horizontally and vertically; that deals with both technical and business issues; and that deals with multiple projects concurrently (see Figure 8-1).

The nature of your role and the context switching required for your position change dramatically when you move from being a tech lead to an architect. This transformation includes the following changes:

- Moving from being primarily department focused to being business unit or even cross business unit focused
- Moving from being technical structure focused to being heavily business focused (new language, new concerns)
- Moving from being highly focused on a few projects to being more lightly focused on many projects
- Moving from being sheltered from most management issues to dealing with management issues directly at multiple levels of the organization

The challenge when switching roles in this way is that the risk of becoming overwhelmed by an onslaught of noncoherent activities is high. The issues that arise come quickly, the context behind the issue may not be self-evident, and the amount of time you have to jump on the grenade is short.

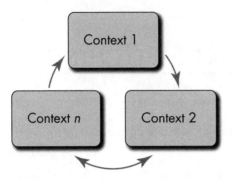

Figure 8-1   Context switching. Leaving the old context and entering the new
context with your full attention is essential, must happen in seconds, and can happen at a rapid pace.

The answers you give in this scenario have some constraints as well:

- They carry the risk of sending one part of the organization off into a
  tailspin in what may seem like a split second.
- They need to be clear and simple.
- They need to be able to be repeated successfully by the person bringing the issue forward to the rest of the organization.
- They need to be consistent. Everyone has to understand where the
  two sides of the bridge being constructed are going to meet in the
  middle. (If the bridge doesn't meet, you are going to get a lot of
  attention that you do not want.)
- They had better not blow the hardware or resource budgets (development or operational) out of the water.
- They had better be aligned with both the strategic and tactical
  nature of the current business environment.

The challenge in dealing with each request effectively is that each person
bringing forward questions and issues has a slightly different context. That
is, each person has

- A different set of assumptions.
- A slightly different language. (You may have a clear understanding
  of the phrases and terms in your own head, but the person making
  the request may not have the same meaning in place.)
- A slightly different goal to achieve. (I really want to use this new
  cool technology; I really want to avoid doing this work of unraveling
  a 25-page if statement that no one really understands and for which

the fear of God strikes anyone brave enough to touch it—the last person who tried failed miserably.)

- A slightly different set of distractions. (Where are my kids playing soccer tonight? Who is going to win that football game tonight? Did I lock the door on the way out of the house today?)

Whenever you are interrupted and you are about to change contexts, you need to understand two things, as depicted in Figure 8-2: (1) the context that you are currently in and (2) the context that you are moving to. Consciously recognizing that you are shifting contexts helps give you the focus you need to be effective.

This chapter shows you how to successfully use context switching as a key soft skill that will enable you to find success as a software architect and help you to maintain some level of sanity.

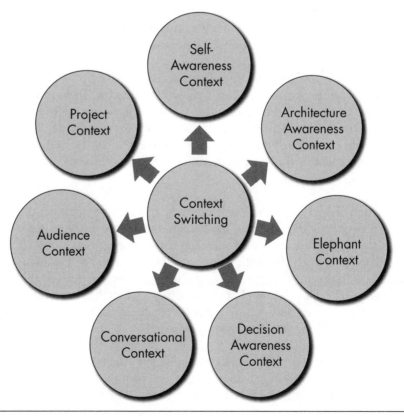

Figure 8-2   Context switching map

SELF-AWARENESS CONTEXT

The first context we focus on is self-awareness. Before you begin switching contexts, you need to know where you are starting.

Be Where You Are

The art of life is to live in the present moment.

—Emmet Fox, Author and Lecturer

For an architect during the course of the day, many quick, out-of-context switches naturally occur that require you to seamlessly transition to a new context. The key to successful context switching is to put behind you what you were just doing (to push it onto your internal stack) and refocus your attention on where you currently are (taking into account the people, their problems, and their surrounding contexts).

Such a context switch can occur as you run into people in the hallway, as you move from one meeting to another, as you answer the phone, as someone enters your office, as you notice a new email. The list goes on and on.

When you sense the need to refocus your attention, take a moment to mentally file away the previous context (you will need to be able to return to it later) and think about the new context (what the person is really asking or talking about). If the person jumps in too quickly for a particular issue and you are not immediately tracking to the new context, ask the individual to start again and give you more background information so both of you will be in the same ballpark.

If you don't have time to deal with a particular issue or request, let the person know quickly that you need to attend to the matter you were just working on. Ask that the individual schedule some time with you later. If it is email or a phone call, deal with it later; avoid the context and the disruption dealing with this missive may cause. If it is important, the person will leave a message. The one exception I normally make is when the phone call comes from an executive: Deal with it immediately, because the executive likely would not be calling you if it wasn't a real issue.

Give the person your full, complete, undivided attention. Your ability to focus on where you are at will allow you to deal with the issue in an efficient manner and, hopefully, put it behind you quickly. Ideally, you will deal with the issue one time and then move on; this outcome means that your time will be less fragmented, and it allows others to move on more quickly.

Be Aware of Your Weaknesses

Sometimes, you may be your own worst enemy. When you need to context-switch a lot, your most basic instincts for how to react and how to approach a problem tend to rise to the top. The challenge is that these decisions and reactions can be a blind spot; that is, your assumptions may not be clearly identified. If you have a tendency to select new technologies or to select known technologies; to procrastinate on making a decision or to jump immediately to a conclusion; to avoid conflict or to be more aggressive under stress—whatever your weaknesses are, you need to be aware of them and be mindful of when and why you are heading down a particular path.

There's More to Life Than Work

Although the daily adrenaline rush of achieving everything that needs to be done and slaying the fire-breathing dragons in your life can be fun, exiting, and addictive, you need to maintain a balance in your life. If you are not careful, you can literally consume yourself.

Your family is far more important than work. When you are at home, leave the BlackBerry in its holster.

Your family is equally affected by the context switches that occur. When you are with them, focus on them and them alone (leave work and other issues at bay; you can deal with that later). Be where you are—you will be happier, and so will your family.

The Myth of Multitasking Efficiency

You can do only one difficult task at a time. At any given time, your mind can only really focus on just one thing; though you can certainly do other tasks that don't require your focused attention, there is a limit to how far you can stretch its multitasking capabilities.

Learn to limit the number of concurrent projects that you oversee at one time. There is a practical constraint on the number of projects you can oversee.

For any project, one of the key elements is to seek dedicated resources. You need the right resources, and when they are dedicated to a task, they can focus solely on the problem at hand and avoid context switching. Every time they need to context switch, a cost is incurred, in the form of time for ramping down and ramping up. The same is true for architecture.

Keep the Adrenaline in Check: Sloooow Down

The pace of life for architects can seem like a frantic dash through each and every week. The hectic nature of the position does a great job of making each day pass quickly. The hurried pace can lull you into a habit of responding quickly to the barrage of questions and decisions that need to be attended to. The challenge is that you need to slow yourself down long enough to ensure that you have a reasonable amount of information on which to base your actions.

The decisions you make may have long-term impacts and may cause confusion throughout the organization if they are not carefully considered. They also need to be in line with the previous decisions that have been made, so that a consistent drumbeat is heard in all of the messages disseminated.

ARCHITECTURAL AWARENESS CONTEXT

The second context addressed here is architectural awareness. The purpose in this case is to be grounded on architectural principles as you switch contexts.

Bring the -Ilities

For an architect, the notion of the -ilities (reliability, scalability, availability, and so on) always needs to be a filter that is applied to what you want to say. These nonfunctional requirements can often help filter out possible solutions quickly and give you a reasonable set of answers that can not only functionally accomplish what the business wants, but also ensure that the parts of the system are accounted for (those things that no one will praise you for managing, but whose omission from consideration will prompt others to quickly find fault).

Seek Proper Coupling and Cohesion

To a great degree, much of architecture addresses various aspects of coupling and cohesion (that is, which things belong together and which things belong apart). When software development occurs, it is so easy to include "just one more thing" on a particular project or software component. It is easy to say, "Okay, just add this one more thing." The challenge is that as these types of incremental changes continue to be introduced, more entropy enters the picture, the cohesion of the component becomes less clear, and its purpose becomes more diluted. As you approve these changes from an architecture perspective, you need to keep firmly in mind the context of the purpose, goal, or vision of the particular piece of software, service, or component.

The same can be said for the distribution of software development tasks within a large development group. When decisions need to be made as to which group should develop a particular piece of functionality, think carefully about the organization impacts of where this functionality will reside. Consider the following questions:

- Who has the best background to implement this functionality?
- Who is going to care if it breaks?
- Who understands the nature of the problem from a domain perspective?
- Who understands the nonfunctional requirements that need to be implemented?
- Who has a relationship with the customers?

As you consider the organization's ecosystem, coupling and cohesion will draw you toward natural boundaries between divisions. Treating all groups in the organization as just a single set of resources does not work and is not a good means of distributing the development work that needs to occur. Just because a particular area doesn't have much to do, that does not mean that they should be the group to take on the next development effort. Decisions in this area may span political battles, however, as different groups vie for valuable development dollars.

Most organizations want to own as much of the problem as they can, which enables them to control their destiny and to effectively work through issues and balance resources within their span of control. The challenge becomes trying balance tactical and strategic needs. For tactical purposes, having a relatively closed project allows you to control scope, balance resources, and manage priorities. It may allow you to meet the necessary deadlines, but may affect the maintenance costs of the project owing to the existence of duplicate software or duplicate data.

From a strategic perspective, building areas of expertise may cause you to distribute the project responsibilities differently. The question, however, remains the same: Can priorities and communication be maintained in such a way that the desired delivery dates and quality measures are met?

When software is organized both from a structural perspective and from an organizational perspective, it will naturally minimize the amount of context switching that is needed between components and groups.

Constantly Build Your Context

For the architect, it is essential to manage by walking around and around and around. You can't have too much information. Being engaged with your teams on a regular, if not on a constant, basis will help you make informed decisions. On large projects, things can move quickly. Knowing what is happening, what is going wrong, and what is going right can help you have a context for managing the next set of decisions that are in the process of chasing you down. It will also prepare you for surprise status requests from executives and others who want an ad hoc debriefing.

You need to be plugged in to what is happening technically and politically. The relationships that two executives have can dramatically affect your ability to execute plans successfully. If they are at odds with each other, that fact may help explain why certain parts of the organization are acting oddly. The strategic directions in which the company is trying to move and the area to which an executive is about to move can play into which requests are made or which issues are questioned.

The challenge is that you will never be fully aware of all of the parameters that are at play for any given day. Even so, the more you are able to stay in sync with the technical organizations and the business organizations, the better you will be able to navigate the road that is immediately in front of you and to reach the goals you are trying to achieve.

ELEPHANT CONTEXT

The third context is simply being aware of the elephant in the room (see Figure 8-3). The purpose of this section is to bring awareness of the need to focus on what is not being said, despite the fact that an issue clearly exists and needs to be brought out into the open.

Figure 8-3 Don't avoid the elephant in the room; everyone knows it's there. Just deal with it.

What Is Not Being Said?

The information that is not on the table is what will kill you. When you are required to switch contexts, the context that you are about to move into has a stage that is already being set. The questions and comments that you hear all have a marketing message associated with them. Be cautious in what you accept as truth. Does the argument being made seem one sided? Rarely are things completely clear-cut; rarely are simple black-and-white considerations apparent. Find out about both sides of the issue. Both sides will try to establish a certain set of assumptions; as the old adage goes, when you assume, you make an ASS out of U and ME.

Once you make a decision, it is likely to be repeated throughout the organization. If you have not considered things carefully, you will be inviting a long string of guests to appear at your doorstep asking if you have considered these other variants, or letting you know there was more to the problem than what was presented, or informing you that another area within the company has chosen a different direction.

Take the time to hear both what is being said and what is not being said. Find out which assumptions are being made, and question these assumptions before you adopt them as part of your decision-making process.

Ask the Hard Questions

Before addressing the elephant in the room, ask yourself the following questions:

- Why are you saying something? What is the driver? What are you trying to avoid?
- What are you personally going to gain? What will you lose?

- Are you really putting everything on the table?
- Are you giving everyone a fair chance to hear the real story?
- Whose decision is this (really)?
- Who needs to be informed about the decision? When do those individuals need to hear about the decision?
- Which contingencies need to be put in place? When do the contingency paths need to be chosen?
- Does this decision matter? Can you decide? What are the ramifications if you decide? If you make a bad decision, can you recover?

Now consider the same questions, but from the perspective of others.

Sometimes dealing with the issues head on is the best approach. Working toward transparency of the context that you maintain as well as the context that others maintain will allow you to resolve issues. This approach may not be fun, but it is highly effective. You need to let others know that you are not attacking them, but rather attacking the problem. As always, use good judgment and avoid offending people, because you will need to work with them tomorrow.

If you don't ask the hard questions now, don't worry: Others will ask later. At that point, of course, you will need to explain why these issues were not addressed earlier.

Deliver the Bad News Early

The earlier you deliver bad news, the earlier it can be dealt with, and the earlier different solutions and approaches can be developed and implemented. By getting a jump and establishing the context of the bad news, you have an opportunity to help shape the resolution of the problem. If you let the bad news escape from your control by procrastinating or out of fear of what others may think, don't worry—the message will get delivered whether you are the messenger or not. If you allow others to frame the information, they will have the opportunity to slant it in a way that may be very difficult to manage later on. Your best course of action is to attack the matter head on and just deal with it. Bad things happen every day—it is how you respond to them that matters.

If They Owned the Company, What Would They Do?

When people come to you for resolution of a problem or a decision, find out if they already know the answer. If they don't, help them think through the various facets of the problem. Sometimes getting petitioners to step back and consider what they would do if they owned the company is an effective way of ensuring that they gain a broader context. Understanding of this context many times makes the answer or decision clear, even if it is not the answer they are looking for.

DECISION AWARENESS CONTEXT

The fourth context is being aware of the decisions that have already been made or already thought through. The purpose of this section is to bring out what knowledge is already known.

Do They Already Have the Problem Solved?

Sometimes when people ask you a question, they are simply asking for confirmation that the problem they have already solved or another group has already solved has been handled correctly. Generally speaking, a working piece of software that does most of what is required is better than building something new.

Take the time to listen, and have the individuals provide the context of what they know, where things are currently at, what needs to be done differently, and which other groups have they talked to. Often, people are looking for permission to do the right thing.

If you are looking to buy a tool, how much are you going to change what it does to successfully do what you need? What are the integration costs? Which defects or assumptions are deeply ingrained into this solution?

The key to successful decision making is to understand the cost of getting there.

As an architect, you have the power to authorize expenditures to be made. You need to spend your capital (financial or political) wisely.

Do They Know Which Alternatives Are Possible?

On any given day, you may be asked a question that at first seems quite innocent: Which technology should I use for this new tool? The direct answer is simple: You have standards, guidelines, or previous norms that should guide you in answering. In reality, the first question you should ask is "Why are you building this new tool?" The next question you may want to ask yourself is "Is there something else that already does this?" Recognize that the first (and natural) response to a problem from a software developer is to build something (something new and independent).

Listening to what individuals are asking for, understanding why they need what they are asking for, and determining the context of the overall problem they are trying to solve will help you guide them to the right answer. Make sure they are aware of other tools or other solutions that already meet their needs; using these existing products can save the company money and minimize the ongoing software maintenance costs.

If developers do suggest purchasing a tool, ask about the licensing costs. If it is an open-source tool, ask about the licensing agreements (restrictions) associated with the tool.

Understanding the constraints that this tool will bring is critical. It may solve today's problem, but prevent you from scaling up in the future, or it may tie you into maintenance upgrades that you are unable to easily perform, leaving you with an orphaned piece of technology.

Have Others Already Weighed in on the Decision?

In many cases, the question being posed now has been asked previously and a decision has been made. Whether you made the original decision or not, you need to be aware of the organizational resilience and boundaries surrounding the decision. Often, once a decision has been made (for good or ill), there is an organizational resistance to change. In some sense, a neuron has been fired and its muscle memory has been established. There are only so many battles that you can successfully take on, so you need to choose your battles wisely.

The issue here is not that you don't want to challenge a previous decision when you feel it is the right thing to do. Rather, the problem is that you cannot challenge everything just because you don't like it. There is an organizational price tag associated with change—make sure you are willing to pay the price for overcoming that change.

Learning to choose your battles carefully can keep you in a politically viable position. If you make too many decisions that go against the grain of the organization, you may see your scope of responsibility reduced or you may start getting more help on your decisions.

Be a Neutral Third Party, Even When It Is a Disadvantage

Architects are put into the role of needing to balance strategic and tactical needs on a daily basis. The technical vision of Nirvana is always appealing and usually seems just out of reach given the current project deadline. The challenge becomes knowing which deadlines and which resource constraints are real. Working closely with your business partners can help determine what the "right" course of action should be. Don't be afraid to ask.

When it comes to making a decision, put everything on the table. You need to operate in the best interest of the business, even if it means your pet project disappears or is radically altered.

CONVERSATIONAL CONTEXT

The fifth context is being aware of the conversational aspects of context switching. This section focuses on the need to personalize the context and make sure the right parties are involved with the context.

Avoid Meetings and Email

Meetings and email are the bane of corporate life. Gather up who you need to make a decision, hold an impromptu meeting, and decide. Capture action items and then follow up with them or, better yet, let project managers do that (they are effective at nagging—following up, that is). The likelihood of success when you meet face to face to make a decision is dramatically higher.

Bring in Others (Now), If Needed

When you are nearing a decision that has a potentially broad impact, bringing in members from other parts of the organization can help solidify the context that has been established for the potential decision. If you can, drop by with the others and hold a quick impromptu meeting. This type of joint decision with all the information on the table is powerful and supportable throughout the organization. The hurdles can be removed before they become public obstacles.

AUDIENCE CONTEXT

The sixth context is being aware of the audience for your decision. Ideally, you will learn to adjust your style of interaction when making a decision based on who you are interacting with.

Know Your Audience

The nature of architecture is such that many different parts of the organization need to interact with it. This leads to the need to communicate clearly and concisely to each of the following groups:

- Executives (vice presidents, chief technology officers, chief information officers, and so on)
- Directors
- Managers
- Developers
- Project managers
- Technology operations
- Business operations
- New product development
- Research and development
- Marketing
- Testing
- Finance

Be Appropriate

Don't supply unnecessary context; it's neither needed nor helpful.

Sometimes Play Good Cop, Bad Cop

Sometimes role playing can help establish a good context for the decisions that need to be considered. Let one person play the good cop (the cooperative person) and the other play the bad cop (the person who brings up the issues and challenges the decision). If need be, flip the roles; this reversal can help people think through the issue from multiple perspectives and gain an appreciation for all of the considerations that went into the decision. It will also help them defend the decision when they bring it back to others within their organization.

Supply Background Information

If people understand the broader context, their willingness to do hard things increases. If they understand what other groups are already contributing, their willingness to do hard things also increases.

PROJECT CONTEXT

The last context to address is which project or projects are involved or may be affected by the decisions you are about to make. Depending on the project, your answers will likely need to change depending on the variables that are at play, such as budget, resources, and assumptions (see Figure 8-4).

Bring a Budget

As you are context switching, you need to be aware of the fixed boundaries around the project. For each project, ask yourself these questions:

- What is the hardware budget?
- How much of the hardware budget has currently been spent?
- What is the lead time for hardware?
- Which people resources are available?
- Which technologies are they familiar with?
- How easily do they adopt new technologies?
- What kind of database capacity is currently available?
- What is the required quality level for the project?
- What is the time frame for fulfilling this request?

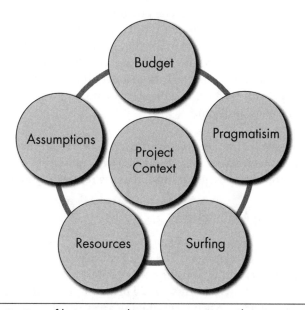

Figure 8-4   Part of being an architect is partnering with project managers and helping them manage the constraints and messaging of a project.

A high-level sense of the boundaries can ensure that you understand the context in which you must respond to particular questions. If a huge strategic project is currently under way, all of your critical resources may be fully dedicated to that effort. As a result, what might normally be possible may become impossible due to the "right" resources not being available. The critical factor in such a case is understanding how much margin is available for each dimension of the problem.

If you make decisions without understanding the constraints, you may fail to deliver the project on time. In general, there is little forgiveness for missing project deadlines, regardless of the reason for the failure.

Bring Pragmatism

As you work through the transition from one context to another, and as you begin listening to what is being requested of you, keep a pragmatic view of what needs to be done.

From a technology perspective, there is always a desire to keep current and maintain a reasonably well-crafted set of software. The challenge is that over time, a natural entropy takes place. Given that most organizations are date driven (they desire to get a product out the door as quickly as possible), the amount of time and effort that can be spent "cleaning house or making upgrades" needs to be well thought out. Is there really a perceived benefit from the changes? Can we really make the dates if we embark on this next "necessary" refactoring? Take time to think through the practical aspects of the decisions being made. Most tasks take longer than we think. Sometimes the complexity that is inherent in a piece of software reflects the complexity of the larger business problem.

If you were paying for the solutions you are about to recommend, would you shell out the money? Nearly everything you say and do is a financial decision for the company—be a good steward of the resources you influence.

Learn to Surf the Avalanche

The architect, by the very nature of his or her job, plays a central role throughout project development. The set of issues you face and your facility in changing contexts and establishing new contexts quickly will determine your ability to be effective in this role. This sea of context switching may make you feel as if you are being engulfed in an avalanche. Learning to surf the avalanche is essential. You always need to know where you are and where you are going even though there is a lot of commotion going on around you.

Seek Out Dedicated Resources

As each context switch occurs during the course of the day, a penalty in efficiency is incurred. You need to mentally shut down what you are currently working on and shift to the new situation that has presented itself. Later, you need to pop the stack (mentally file away anything important from the situation that has concluded and reestablish the context that you previously were focused on).

The more dedicated that you can keep the team working on your software projects, the more likely that the software they produce will be cohesive, have a higher quality, and be completed on time.

With each context switch that occurs during the day in the process of dealing with a variety of projects, a natural prioritization occurs. The team members will likely either seek to do the things they like or seek to keep the squeaky wheel quiet (the project manager who nags them the most).

For the sake of both yourself as an architect and the teams you interact with (including your business partners), seek to gain dedicated resources and maintain a sharp project focus to enable the best product to be delivered.

Which Assumptions Are You Making?

The hardest things for you to lay on the table are the things that you are internally assuming about the project. Be aware of your tendencies and keep them in check. These assumptions contain information that may come back to haunt you unintentionally. What really could go wrong? If those things happen, how will you recover? Is it a documented risk or assumption? Show transparency for the assumptions you make.

BECOMING A CONTEXT-AWARE ARCHITECT

The road to becoming a context aware architect begins with the following steps:

- Context 1: Self-awareness
    - Be where you are.
    - Be aware of your weaknesses.
    - There's more to life than work.
    - Don't fall prey to the myth of multitasking efficiency.
    - Keep the adrenaline in check: slow down.

- Context 2: Architectural awareness
  - Bring the -ilities.
  - Seek proper coupling and cohesion.
  - Constantly build your context.
- Context 3: Elephant awareness
  - What is not being said?
  - Ask yourself and others the hard questions; if you don't, those questions will just get asked later.
  - Deliver the bad news early.
  - Ask others what they would do if they owned the company.
- Context 4: Decision awareness
  - Do they already have the problem solved?
  - Do they know which alternatives are possible?
  - Have others already weighed in on the decision?
  - Be a neutral third party, even when it is to your disadvantage.
- Context 5: Conversational awareness
  - Avoid meetings and email; prefer face-to-face conversations.
  - Bring others in if needed (now).
- Context 6: Audience awareness
  - Know your audience.
  - Be appropriate.
  - Sometimes play "good cop, bad cop."
  - Supply background information.
- Context 7: Project awareness
  - Be conscious of the budgets you need to operate within.
  - Be pragmatic in your approach.
  - Learn to surf the avalanche.
  - Seek dedicated resources.
  - Know the assumptions you are making.

Learning to be context aware comes naturally to some. For me, I need to think about it. I need to consciously consider which other variables might be at play. I need to actively look for assumptions that are being made that could derail the decision being made. The chief element of becoming context aware is to realize when your context is switching.

BIBLIOGRAPHY

Maxwell, John C. (1997). *Becoming a Person of Influence: How to Positively Impact the Lives of Others.* Thomas Nelson.

Patterson, Kerry; Grenny, Joseph; McMillan, Ron; Switzler, Al. (2002). *Crucial Conversations: Tools for Talking When Stakes Are High.* McGraw-Hill.

PART III

BUSINESS SKILLS

Information technology and business are becoming inextricably inter-woven. I don't think anybody can talk meaningfully about one without the talking about the other.

—Bill Gates, Founder of Microsoft

Part III focuses on the four essential business skills for an architect. These chapters explore the set of skills that will allow you to truly stand out among the field of architects for your business—based on your ability to help drive the business forward and grow in the context of business needs, not just your technical prowess. The chapters in Part III cover the following topics:

- **Chapter 9: Business Knowledge.** Your ability to truly understand the language of business and the drivers that come into play when making tough decisions to enable the business to grow.
- **Chapter 10: Innovation.** Your ability to bring new and innovative ideas forward that aren't just technically "cool," but rather facilitate revenue growth and sustained viability.
- **Chapter 11: Pragmatism.** Your ability to make decisions that are the best ones for the company as a whole, rather than simply promoting the latest and greatest technology as a requirement for the next project.
- **Chapter 12: Vision.** Your ability to see where the business is going, to help formulate where the business could go, and to help the business safely navigate the treacherous waters of technology projects.

Your relationship skills and personal skills will help formulate a solid foundation that enables you to successfully execute the many diverse tasks required of an architect. However, business skills are the top tier of skills that you need to differentiate yourself within your organization (see Figure P3-1 on the next page).

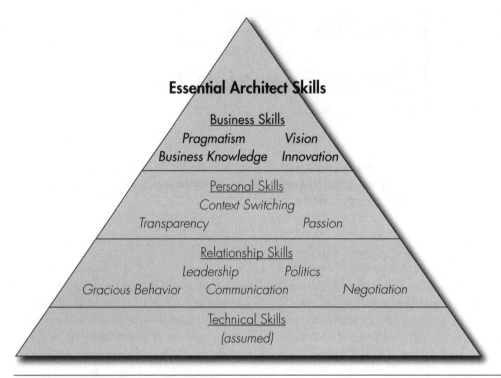

Figure P3-1 Essential architect skills: business skills

Chapter 9

BUSINESS KNOWLEDGE

Your earning ability today is largely dependent upon your knowledge, skill, and your ability to combine that knowledge and skill in such a way that you contribute value for which customers are going to pay.

—Brian Tracy, Author/Speaker, *The Way to Wealth*

Of central importance is the changing nature of competitive advantage—not based on market position, size, and power as in times past, but on the incorporation of knowledge into all of an organization's activities.

—Leif Edvinsson, Swedish Intellectual Capital Expert

If you work just for money, you'll never make it, but if you love what you're doing and you always put the customer first, success will be yours.

—Ray Kroc, American Businessman

Software architecture is all about building systems that meet the business's needs. However, it is easy to get caught up in the frenzy of reveling in the technical details that surround building the system.

Most software architects achieved their position through excellence in technical details. They were able to synthesize that knowledge in a manner that allowed them to complete the following tasks:

- Deliver components of a system in a timely manner
- Unwind complex technical issues
- Translate requirements into working software
- Oversee the work of others
- Mentor others on their team and on other teams
- Communicate with management, technical staff, and business representatives
- Model information
- Maintain technical "currency"
- Be aware of and understand technology trends

These capabilities, along with a glimmer of soft skills, attract the attention of management and prompt executives to begin considering an individual for an architectural position.

The challenge for the architect is being able to see the big picture: No matter how technically awesome a particular system is, if it is not able to meet the needs of the business (both functional and operational needs), the software is of no use. To minimize this risk, a shift in focus needs to occur. Specifically, the architect cannot be solely focused on the technical aspects of system construction, but rather must incorporate a solid understanding of customer value (what is the real customer problem you are helping solve?) in conjunction with business value (how does this help the company make money?) when considering the true worth of the proposed software architecture.

This chapter shows you how to pursue and incorporate business knowledge into the everyday world of software architecture. Gaining business knowledge will require you to understand businesses generally (what all that business jargon means, such as "ROI"), understand your company (what "special sauce" your company brings to its employees, the products it makes, and its history), understand your customers (who buys your products and why), and, finally, how all of these areas intersect to create the domain (how all of the elements fit together). Figure 9-1 illustrates this interweaving of business knowledge and software architecture.

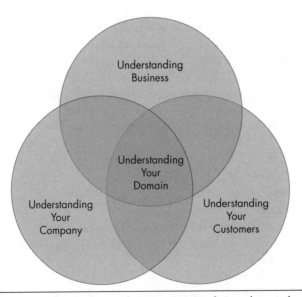

Figure 9-1   To understand your domain, you need to understand your company, its customers, and the business.

UNDERSTANDING BUSINESS

The business of business is making money. Taking time out of your busy schedule to learn the language of business can greatly improve your ability to hear what your business partners (marketing, sales, and so on) and the executives higher up on the organizational chart are saying. This improved understanding of the business language will help you produce the products that the business really needs. It will enable you to make mirco-level business decisions every day that will help improve your company's business proposition with its (and your) customers.

Marketing, Finance (ROI), and Sales

In the world of large-scale software development, marketing, finance, and sales are often distant, nebulous entities. We hear about the denizens of these departments, and we occasionally talk to them, but their direct presence is not felt on a daily basis.

The one common strand between all of these areas, including technology, is the need to ensure that customer demands for value are met or exceeded. The job of marketing is to create an environment in which perceived customer value is easily recognized by existing and potential customers. The job of finance is to ensure that the cost structure associated with the product or family of products is able to maintain the financial health and growth expectations of the company. The job of sales is to connect customers to the right products on the stage that marketing has helped prepare and within the price structures that finance has helped to set.

As shown in Figure 9-2, the parts of a business, although they may appear to be working in opposition to one another, usually mesh together like well-oiled gears. In doing so, they help deliver the return on investment (ROI) that is needed to drive the business to a profitable state.

Usually, a few key financial metrics determine whether a project is successful. First and foremost is the ROI. This is basically the amount of profit that will be generated from the project divided by the amount that will be invested into the project. For example, companies may set a performance bar specifying what they hope to achieve from a particular investment, such as a 20% (profit/investment)[1] ROI (year over year) for the capital that will be invested.

---

1. www.solutionmatrix.com/return-on-investment.html

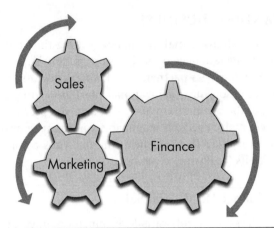

Figure 9-2 Sales, marketing, and finance personnel must work together.

Depending on the nature of the project, the company may choose to raise or lower this bar. For instance, if it is a strategic project, the organization may decide to accept a lower rate of return. Perhaps the project will position the company favorably in the overall marketplace, or perhaps the new capabilities associated with the project will enable the company to complete future projects in a more efficient manner; both considerations may warrant accepting a lower ROI. Conversely, for a tactical project, the company may push the required ROI up to 30%, 40%, or even 70%.

From a financial perspective, take time to learn how your company makes investment decisions. Doing so will help you understand the financial nature of the project and the reasons why certain questions are being asked when a project is being evaluated for investment purposes.

From a marketing and sales perspective, take time to understand the following issues:

- How do your organization's marketing and sales personnel segment your customers?
- What is the key value proposition for each market segment?
- How do the products you help develop fit into this strategy?
- Which segments is the company trying to grow, and how?
- Who makes the buying decisions within each of the markets?
- What is this market's sensitivity to price?

- Are your products considered premium products, or are they perceived as value oriented?
- Who are your chief competitors in each market segment?
- Are your products considered market leaders? If so, why? If not, why not?

As you begin to sense the basis on which the business is evaluating each investment decision and how it is positioning the products you develop within the marketplace, you can take a harder look at the architectural and design decisions you are making. Think about the following issues:

- Are the decisions you are making in alignment with the financial, marketing, and sales goals of the company?
- Are you allowing for future architectural changes in your products that are aligned with the company's strategic direction?
- Is the product you are working on considered a cash cow?
- If so, is the company looking for major changes or just minor changes to fund new development areas?

This type of thinking allows you to become a partner with the business. It also helps your colleagues in other areas of the business gain insight into the impacts of what they wish to accomplish from a technology perspective.

Consider Getting a Business Degree

One of the best ways to learn what is important to the business is to become knowledgeable about the broader business environment. Take the time to read at least a few business books on the topics of marketing, finance, and sales. (See the "Additional Resources" section for a list of recommended books.) Also, consider taking a few seminars on business-related topics.

My own natural areas of interest lie with technology. I love to read books, magazines, blogs, and forums on, and go to conferences about, technology. Keeping up to date in these areas takes no effort on my part; it aligns with my innate passion for technology. The business side of this world, although interesting, does not hold the same sway on my attention.

Even so, I recognize that success in technology can be truly attained only when the business is successful. Our futures (both technology and business) are dependent and intertwined.

As a technologist, when you begin to listen to the requests from new product development or marketing personnel, you quickly realize that these colleagues are not from your "tribe." They do not speak the same language as you do. Their understanding of technology is limited—but their understanding of customers and the ways in which those customers use your products is impressive.

Because these business-oriented personnel don't speak the same language as software developers do, the communication barrier can sometimes be a bit thick. Only part of the message that they are trying to convey to you is likely to make it through your internal translator. They may begin using terms such as "return on investment" and "expense versus capital," or they may delve into domain-specific lingo. Your mind sees these words and phrases, but quickly drops them in search of a message that you can relate to. Although this form of communication is commonplace, it is not effective in translating the true intent of the business owners to your internal map of what is being requested.

My interest in improving communication between myself (as a technology representative) and the business crowd drove me to seek to learn their language, thereby enabling me to become part of their tribe, or at least a proficient translator. The approach that I determined was best for me in immersing myself in the world of business was to seek an advanced business degree. I did my research, and it kept pointing toward an MBA. Although an MBA would potentially meet my goal, I wanted something that would have more of technology slant to it—something related to the effects of business on technologists.

I eventually enrolled in the Management of Technology program at the University of Minnesota, which offered the mix of classes I was looking for. Half of this program was dedicated to classic MBA-type classes from the Carlson School of Management—classes such as accounting, marketing, operations, and new product development. The other half of the program focused on the management of technology; it included classes such as strategic management, managing intellectual property, pivotal technologies, technology foresight, and managing technical innovation. I decided to focus on strategic management as my area of specialization.

As the courses progressed, it felt as if I had a series of increasingly better glasses to improve my business vision. It was amazing how I was able to start hearing what the business was actually saying regarding the financial aspects of the operation. Words that business-focused personnel had previously said would simply go in one ear and out the other—but now they had clear meaning. The MBA program also gave me less apprehension about delving more into the business side of technology.

UNDERSTANDING YOUR COMPANY

Once you gain an understanding of the basics of business, the next major challenge is for you to familiarize yourself with your company's products and their value proposition to your customers. This relationship is what pays your salary. Learn to pay close attention to this linkage: What are your customers really paying for? Has this always been their value proposition, or has it changed over time?

Know Your Product's Value Proposition

Great ideas have no value. What you need is the money to go with them.

—Professor Tim Richardson

It is relatively easy to come up with a mountain of surface-level great ideas. The challenge is to take these ideas and unearth the underlying customer value proposition that an idea will cling to for dear life.

Once you establish a clear linkage between the idea and the customer value proposition (ideally with real customer input), getting the business to choose to invest (the hard part) will be a relatively straightforward process (see Figure 9-3). Many times, if you listen closely to customers' input,

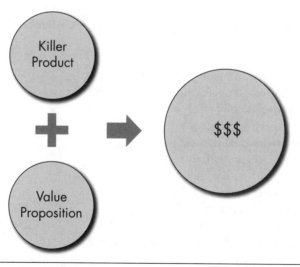

Figure 9-3   Know your company's value proposition: Live it, embrace it, enhance it.

they will tell you what they want—that is, what they are willing to pay for—because it would provide them significant value.

Know How Your Company Makes Money

As you begin to better understand the role of finance, sales, and marketing, take the time to learn how your company actually makes money:

- Does it rely on recurring revenue such as subscriptions?
- Does it rely on ancillary revenues?
- Does it rely on advertising revenues?
- Does it rely on product-derived revenues?
- Does it rely on services-derived revenues?
- Does it rely on revenues from ecosystems such as an affiliate sales channel?[2]

Recognizing the revenue model or combination of revenue models that your company depends on will help you better understand which architectural styles are appropriate to support the model.

Understand Your Company's History/Culture

There is a story behind every company. This epic tale shapes people's thinking about how you get recognized, how you get promoted, how customer complaints are dealt with—in general, what is acceptable and unacceptable behavior. Taking the time to learn this background helps you become a member in full standing with the tribe. Look and listen for the following information:

- How did the company come into existence?
- Which great struggles did it overcome in the past?
- Who have its chief rivals been?
- What are its great accomplishments?
- Who are its great heroes?
- Who are its great villains?
- How is conflict normally handled?
- Where does innovation begin?
- What have been some epic failures?
- How have the failures been perceived?
- Which kinds of risks are deemed acceptable?

---

2. http://sixteenventures.com/7-SaaS-Revenue-Streams-with-Details.pdf

- What are perceived to be some of the great successes within the company?
- What are the chief elements of that success?

UNDERSTANDING YOUR CUSTOMERS

The customers are really the stars of the show. In a real sense, technology is a supporting actor in a larger play—the one that focuses on the customer. Who are those customers? What do they or their businesses do? How do they make money? What value do you bring to them? Why do they prefer your company's products or services over those offered by your competitors?

Consider Going on a Customer Visit, Sales Call, or Helping Staff a Booth at a Trade Show

The best way to get to know your customers is to actually meet them, talk to them, and hear what they have to say. So often in the world of software development, we must deal with proxies of proxies who claim to represent the interests of the true end customer.

The challenge in such a case is the classical morphing of information as it travels from person to person. The horse that ate the apple becomes the cow that jumped over the moon. Although most people act in the best interest of their customer, they inevitably color the images that are portrayed from their own vantage point. Your attempts to gain a true understanding of the domain becomes challenging in this bias-prone environment.

From a business perspective, the task of getting technologists up to speed can truly be expensive from multiple perspectives:

- The cost of traveling to a customer site, which can involve plane fares, overnight travel, car rentals, meals, and so on
- The cost of preparing the technologist for the visit
- The cost in time of the sales person who is trying to make his or her quota
- The loss in productivity for the time you are visiting customers versus developing software
- The Dilbert effect that plagues most technologists:
    - The risk of unknowingly revealing strategic efforts that the company is trying to keep under wraps to surprise the competition
    - The risk of saying things that are misinterpreted
    - The risk of revealing a lack of knowledge

If you ever get the chance to go on a customer visit, say yes. Before you go, however, do some customer research:

- Which products does the customer make?
- How does it make these products?
- Which markets is the customer in?
- How much revenue does the company make?
- How much revenue does the division you will visit make?
- How does the customer sell its product?
- What, if any, advertising does the customer do?
- Which products from your company does the customer use?
- How long has it been a customer of your company?
- Which challenges does the customer face?
- What is its strategic vision?
- Will your company's products help the customer achieve its vision?
- Can the sales team brief you before the visit takes place?

This type of information can usually be found at the company's Web site and in its annual report; it may also be gathered by talking to some of your company's sales and marketing representatives. If you have any burning questions, check in advance if it is okay to ask them. The thing you don't want to do is to surprise the sales person whom you are accompanying.

When you go, be sure to follow these guidelines:

- Be gracious, well-mannered, and appreciative.
- Listen. Hear what the customer's representatives are saying; hear the words (this is the domain language your system should be built upon).
- Dress appropriately. Ask the sales person in advance what "appropriate" is in this case.
- Follow the lead of the sales person you are accompanying.
- Ask any preapproved questions if the opportunity presents itself.
- Watch how the customer uses your product.
- Listen for suggestions that would improve your product.
- Listen for areas in which the customer's representatives praise your product.
- Take notes.
- Smile and be friendly.
- Stand up and sit up straight. Shoulders back—you don't want to look like a slug.
- Be alert and pay attention.

When you return:

- Send "thank you" notes to all of the people within your company who took time out of their busy schedules to make the customer visit happen. The company went out of its way to invest in you. Be grateful, and recognize that the visit gave you an opportunity to become a more customer-knowledgeable employee.
- Write a trip report, even if it is just for yourself. Such documentation helps you remember all of the valuable information that you gathered.
- Look for opportunities to use the information you have learned.
- Look for opportunities to share your new-found insight with others.

Consider Watching Usability Studies, Product Concept Interviews, or Other Customer Product Evaluations

For key products, companies will typically engage users early on in product concept development to help the company better understand where its customers are at today, to understand which challenges they face, and to understand how the proposed product concept may help solve a pressing problem.

As the product moves further along the development pipeline, the company may perform usability and other studies to help determine whether the product is intuitively usable, whether it is efficient in the functionality it provides, whether it projects the image desired by users, and whether the product matches the brand that is being built or currently exists.

These types of interviews are often taped or conducted in settings with one-way mirrors to allow others to observe what is being done or said. If you have ever watched one of your products being evaluated, it is truly a humbling experience. Things that you believed were simple and intuitive turn out to be just the opposite. Brand perceptions you believed to be apparent are missing. The sequence of steps to accomplish certain tasks is not easily navigated.

All in all, you will walk away with a desire to listen more closely to what is being said from the product development and marketing staff. You will realize that your limited view of the world may be just that—limited. You may also learn that the still, small voice that urged you to speak up when you saw something during the development of the product matches your users' expectations, and that you should have been a little bolder in expressing your ideas or concerns earlier.

The good thing is that you can learn this information prior to your ship date and adjust the product accordingly.

As always, architects need to be partners with many different facets of the business—the operative word here is "partner." Look for ways that you can help improve the products that you oversee and learn to understand your customers from multiple perspectives.

Consider Using Agile Techniques

One of the great benefits of agile software techniques is their emphasis on customer involvement. This involvement can involve the creation of customer personas that may aid the team in better understanding the rationale behind the story cards as they are developed. It also allows the customer to get immediate feedback on the work that is being done. Agile development does require a higher level of involvement and time commitment, but the results can be truly spectacular, especially with respect to defect rates and desired functionality ending up in the final product.

UNDERSTANDING YOUR DOMAIN

The final area of business knowledge relates to domain knowledge: How does all of this fit together? Is there a way for you to model this integration?

Gather Domain Knowledge

One of the most important things for me as an architect is to familiarize myself with the domain in which I am working. I need to immerse myself in the language of the customer to the point where the language is natural, and I understand the basic nuances of what is being said.

The words used can serve as the basis of a logical model to understand the major components of how customers see their world. They can help to establish both the nouns (the things that will eventually live in the system) and the verbs (the functionality that the system will eventually need to provide). In many respects, software systems should basically be virtual representations/metaphors of the customer's world.

The primary ways that I begin to establish domain knowledge are through interviews and online research. During the interview or research process, I am usually looking for the following data:

- Unique words and phrases that represent things (the nouns/entities)
- The actions that are performed on or by the nouns
- The number of each noun
- The relationship between the nouns:
    - Are these parent/child types of relationships?
    - Are these associative relationships?
    - Are these component (part-of) relationships?
- The kinds of attributes used to describe the nouns
- The people involved with this domain and its entities
- The organization of these people
- The kinds of activities that these people do
- The sequence of activities that they perform
- The way that they know when they are done
- The critical decisions that need to be made

These data can then be used to formulate models that visually represent the information that has been gathered. The users, with a little help from you, should be able to help validate the logical information.

Modeling a domain in this way should improve your ability to communicate with your user community or the proxies who represent your users. Your ability to speak their language will make it much easier for you to communicate with other members of this domain as well. In many respects, you will become adopted into their tribe.

Always look to validate the assumptions you make with respect to the model. Occasionally, important subtleties may arise that are worth capturing or minor defects may be identified that should be corrected.

These models can also be used by others on your team as a means of gaining a better understanding of the user community.

Note that you may have multiple user communities to take into account. For instance, the language that finance personnel uses will be different from the language of marketing personnel, which again will be different from that of your end-state customers.

Knowing who you are talking to and adjusting your language to match that of your conversational partner will help you become a better architect. Your new tribe will appreciate the fact that you are trying to speak their language, even if the end result is a little choppy.

Understand Your Domain in the Business Context

As you learn to create domain models, one of the most important aspects is to begin crafting the model within the context of your business needs. That is, even though many interesting domain objects may exist from a true domain perspective, some may have no relevance for your business. In addition, there may be several business-specific domain objects that do not exist in the real world, but are, in fact, essential for your business to operate.

HELP THE BUSINESS BETTER UNDERSTAND TECHNOLOGY

Part of the job of an architect is not only to work toward gaining business knowledge, but also to share technology knowledge with the larger business. Your business partners may have little or no technology experience, and they are even less likely to have any software development experience.

Your job as a business partner should include taking the time to help the more business-oriented personnel understand the technology impacts of the decisions they are making (see Figure 9-4). What are the performance implications, the quality implications, the hardware sizing implications, and so on?

Help your business peers understand the pros and cons of each decision. Explain what you believe is the best decision and why. It is okay if business personnel don't take your recommendation, but you should still provide this information as a means of helping balance out the wide range of competing interests that are attempting to shape a project early during its conception.

Figure 9-4   Help the business-oriented personnel understand how developers think about the problem. Sharing this knowledge helps people understand the language of technology and enhances your ability to communicate with one another.

You need to have a sense of who the critical stakeholders are with respect to a particular project. If you communicate with only a handful of the stakeholders on a regular basis, you may fail to communicate key decisions to the others in a timely manner. You may be, by the process of omission, causing yourself some serious future headaches.

If the stakeholders are being told about a decision rather being part of the decision-making process, they may be inclined to challenge the decision in a rather public manner. They have no skin in the game. Perhaps a reorganization of the business meant that they were not part of the original business product concept formulation, and they simply choose not to accept the assumptions that were made.

As reorganizations occur within the company, be aware of the new political alignments that are being formed and adjust your strategies accordingly. You may not be able to maneuver out of every political battle, but with a little effort you can certainly make your architectural life a little saner.

BECOMING A BUSINESS-SAVVY ARCHITECT

The road to becoming a business-savvy architect begins with the following steps:

- Understanding business:
    - Learn about marketing, finance, ROI, and sales.
    - Get a business degree.
- Understanding your company:
    - Know your product's value proposition.
    - Know how your company makes money.
    - Understand your company's history and culture.
- Understanding your customers:
    - Go on a customer visit or sales call.
    - Participate in customer usability studies, and watch product concept interviews and evaluations.
    - Use agile processes.
- Understanding your domain:
    - Gather domain knowledge.
    - Understand your domain in the business context.
- Helping the business better understand technology.

Learning to be a business-savvy architect can greatly help your effectiveness in working with the business side of software development. Focusing on the gathering of business knowledge over the years has helped me become an effective architect. Of course, everything does not run smoothly all of the time, but this integration of the business and software sides has enabled me to work closely with the business in establishing pragmatic solutions that meet the business needs.

BIBLIOGRAPHY

Bick, Julie. (1999). *The Microsoft Edge: Insider Strategies for Building Success.* Simon & Schuster.

Cooper, Robert G. (2001). *Winning at New Products: Accelerating the Process from Idea to Launch.* Basic Books.

Kawasaki, Guy (2008). *Reality Check: The Irrelevant Guide to Outsmarting, Outmanaging, and Outmarketing Your Competition.* Portfolio.

Kilts, James M.; Mandfredi, John F.; Lorber, Rober. (2007). *Doing What Matters: How to Get Results That Make a Difference: The Revolutionary Old-Fashioned Approach* [Audio CD]. Random House Audio.

Marcus, Alfred. (2005). *Management Strategy: Achieving Sustained Competitive Advantage.* McGraw-Hill.

Marcus, Alfred. (2006). *Winning Moves: Cases in Strategic Management.* Marsh Publications.

Ross, Jeanne W.; Weill, Peter; Robertson, David C. (2006). *Enterprise Architecture as Strategy: Creating a Foundation for Business Execution.* Harvard Business School Press.

Schroeder, Alice. (2008). *The Snowball: Warren Buffet and the Business of Life* [Audio CD]. Random House.

Chapter 10

INNOVATION

Innovation distinguishes between a leader and a follower.

—Steve Jobs, Founder of Apple Computer

Innovation is the ability to see change as an opportunity—not a threat.

—Albert Einstein

Don't confuse the art of the possible with the art of the profitable.

—David Tansley

Capital isn't so important in business. Experience isn't so important. You can get both these things. What is important is ideas. If you have ideas, you have the main asset you need, and there isn't any limit to what you can do with your business and your life.

—Harvey Firestone

Innovating is simply my favorite aspect of being an architect.

One of the chief responsibilities of an architect is to pursue pragmatic innovation. Putting these two concepts next to each other may seem oxymoronic, but in reality it is an approach for achieving innovation in a manner that attempts to continually deliver business value while actively pursuing a vision.

As an architect, you will typically be overbooked from a resource allocation perspective. For example, I normally have 30% to 40% more work than I can possibly do. This amount is effective from a resource allocation perspective—I never have to worry that there might be a minute in the workday that cannot be focused on resolving a particular issue. The challenge is to prioritize these tasks. The daily grind of pursuing multiple high-priority projects naturally gates the amount of innovation (think risk) that I want to pursue at any given time.

The flip side is that without actively pursuing a vision, the amount of future work could become unsustainable and turn into mundane drudgery. I simply need to innovate to maintain my interest level in the work that I do.

If the project doesn't grab me, I am unlikely to be engaged in the work that needs to be done. For me, that means finding ways that I can incrementally lay the infrastructure for a vision across multiple projects. No project is likely to be able to bear the weight or full cost of getting to the vision in a single movement.

This chapter focuses on ways to pursue and incorporate innovation into the everyday world of software architecture.

INNOVATION DEFINED

According to the Australian Research Council, "Innovation is the process that translates knowledge into economic growth and social well-being. It encompasses a series of scientific, technological, organizational, financial and commercial activities."[1] For the purposes of architecture, this definition encompasses the essence of what innovation means. Innovation is more than just coming up with a novel idea. Novelty does not serve the business well when it does not have the prospect of contributing to the financial well-being of a company or organization. Instead, innovation is the work entailed in translating that idea into an economic force.

According to Joseph Tidd, John Bessant, and Keith Pavitt, there are four types of innovation (commonly known as the "four P's"):

- *Product innovation—changes in the things (products or services) that an organization offers*
- *Process innovation—changes in the ways in which those products or service are created and delivered*
- *Position innovation—changes in the context in which the products or services are introduced*
- *Paradigm innovation—changes in the underlying mental model that frames what the organization do.*[2]

---

1. www.arc.gov.au/general/glossary.htm
2. Tidd, Joseph; Bessant, John; Pavitt, Keith. (2005). *Managing Innovation: Integrating Technological, Market and Organizational Change.* John Wiley & Sons.

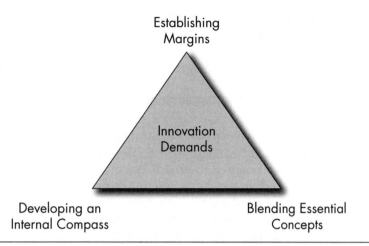

Figure 10-1   Innovation is based on establishing margins, developing an internal compass, and blending essential concepts.

This chapter focuses on three key aspects of innovation (see Figure 10-1):

- **Establishing margin,** which allows you think openly and freely in a safe space that's free from negativity
- **Developing an internal compass,** which enables you to set a course based on your own bearings
- **Blending essential concepts,** which is the ability to recognize and combine old ideas and new ideas that enhance the overall value

ESTABLISHING MARGINS

The first area to address for innovation is to establish margins. Margins are needed in many different areas—margins in time, margins from negativity, margins from existing systems. Essentially, extra space must be set aside for the activity of innovation.

Finding Margins

The ability to innovate depends on having some amount of spare time. You absolutely must have time to step back and think. If you are completely consumed by the daily operations of keeping the current systems running, you will not have the right atmosphere to enable discovery. Instead, you will focus on the next fire, and then the next fire after that—basically, you are just working to keep the lights on.

Although innovation can occur in a bubble to some extent, you need the operational support of the business to conceptually develop, build, test, and roll out the new solutions. Unless you gain the operational support of the business upfront, you are in for a long battle trying to get the solution out to the market:

- Without some degree of isolation, the development staff will naturally focus on the immediate operational fires that are in front of them. This fire fighting is likely to gain them quick praise, whereas the new development is a longer-term recognition process. Ideally, if you can have dedicated staff producing this new product, you can get the focus you need to do the development in a timely fashion. Over the long term, if you don't have some amount of rotation in this area, this static nature can also turn into an issue: You will lose the operational concerns that are necessary to put in the right quality measures to avoid high maintenance costs over the long run.
- Your business partners are likely to adopt an adversarial stance toward taking on new commitments if this effort was not included in their budgetary plans. This kind of executive bartering is likely to be the death of innovation, as it dampens any initiative to take risks and look at new and innovative solutions. Your partners are most likely already being pressed to reduce their expenses, and such commitments will force them to move in the wrong direction.
- Marketing and sales personnel are probably the most likely parties to be supportive of the effort, as innovation will directly help them address customer needs. The challenge is to align the rest of the organization with this perspective.
- New solutions will tend to be more prone to errors and have higher support needs during initial rollout. In many respects, rolling out a new innovative product likely will require significant amounts of resources, both planned and unplanned.

All of these concerns speak to a critical element in fostering innovation: the need for adequate margins. You need time up front to think innovatively, and throughout the process, you need time for things to go wrong and to have a chance to learn, adapt, and recover (see Figure 10-2).

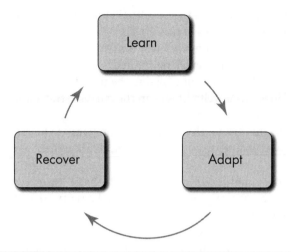

Figure 10-2   Establishing adequate margins enables you to have the space needed to learn, adapt, and recover without drawing excessive attention to these false starts. It enables the organization to incubate—and eventually hatch—ideas.

Innovate at the Edge

Sometimes when you innovate, you make mistakes.

—Steve Jobs, Founder of Apple Computer

Innovation by its very nature is a venture into the world of the unknown. The opportunity for things to go wrong is high. That doesn't mean you should cower in the corner in fear of innovation. Rather, it simply means you need to have a realistic sense of what you are approaching and keep others' expectations properly set. If you sell the innovation in its early phases as the answer to all problems and a sure thing, you are destined for a bad outcome sometime in the future.

When contemplating innovations for a particular area (usually, they hit me out of the blue—sometimes as the culmination of multiple conversations, or sometimes as a thought that jars me awake), the process usually begins with a novel idea. The next step is to figure out how to best capture the novel idea. You will want to answer at least the following questions for intellectual property (IP) protection reasons:

- What is the essence of the novelty that makes it unique?
- Are there alternatives to this novelty?
- Are there ways to improve the novelty?
- Where can this novel idea be applied?
- What are the impacts of applying the novelty there?
- How does this novelty fit within the current strategic vision? (It may completely undermine it.)
- How might this novelty benefit the company? (This understanding will give you a sense of who you should talk to next.)

The span from initial novel idea to some form of business manifestation may take months or even years. Be patient: These types of things tend to take time to mature.

Be cautious with whom you share any ideas that have potential IP implications; ideas that have been shared publicly may lose their chance at being patented. Document your ideas (and be sure to give credit to all those who contributed to the ideas' development in your documentation), do some prior art research, and begin the necessary legal steps (such as getting a provisional patent if you feel a patent is warranted).

Novel ideas can be disruptive to things that are currently working smoothly and are making the company a lot of money (or at least not costing the company much in the way of maintenance dollars). Let pragmatism guide you in this realm when you are contemplating where to introduce this novelty: You don't necessarily want to upset the apple cart.

Look for ways to introduce the innovation near the edge of the system (see Figure 10-3), someplace where its introduction will not be disruptive and where, when it fails (and it will), the cloud of dust from your crash will not be as visible to everyone. This initial relegation of the innovation to the organizational fringes will give you an opportunity to learn, adjust, and try again in a peaceful environment.

What Would You Do? (Given No Constraints, Don't Try to Posture)

When we work on problems, we often constrain ourselves to the family of solutions that are comfortable within our business context. It is the safe place to roam. Unfortunately, this kind of thinking can severely limit your ability to uncover the real innovative solutions that can place you a step ahead of the competition.

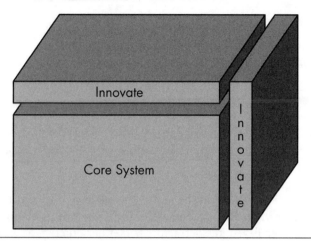

Figure 10-3 Innovating at the edges of the system causes less disruption and provides the incubation time needed for new ideas to grow peacefully.

One approach to overcome this tendency is to contemplate what you would do if you had no constraints, no one to answer to. When we open up our minds, we can begin to explore the vast landscape of possibilities.

Later on, when we want to evaluate feasibility of the various approaches, we can become more critical in our analysis. The point at this time is to focus on discovery—the world of the possible.

Encourage Others to Think and Be Open

On all of my projects, I have one golden rule that I ask those on the project to follow: Think. I don't really care if people make mistakes; we all make them. Rather, I am simply looking for my teammates to have a reason for what they did—laziness is not acceptable.

Ideally, we will learn from the mistake, improve our knowledge, and move on—no harm, no foul. It is okay to make a mistake today; it's not okay to make the same mistake tomorrow.

Implementing a vision is not a simple recipe. It requires a persistent sense of navigation. As an architect, you cannot be everywhere on a project, so you need others to own the work they are doing. Basically, you want to enable your team members to innovate locally.

Be Prepared for the Naysayers

When you innovate, you've got to be prepared for everyone telling you you're nuts.

—Larry Ellison, Founder of Oracle

As your idea nears the end of its path to success (and especially if it hits a few bumps along the way), be prepared for those who wish to kill the idea or at least revel in its flaws. Their reasons may vary, but these negative voices always seem to show up.

Keep a positive attitude. Wish the naysayers well and move on. There really isn't much you can do. Responding in kind will do nothing except hurt you. Once success is achieved, the detractors will either quietly go away or claim to have been believers the whole time.

Be cautious about compromising your vision. If you give away too much of it, the dwindling scope will demotivate you and diminish the passion you have for pursuing the vision.

Avoid the Naysayers and Find a Safe Place to Think

The essential part of creativity is not being afraid to fail.

—Edwin H. Land

Once the naysayers have presented themselves, avoid them if at all possible—the seeds of doubt that they plant can dramatically sap your energy and confidence. By avoiding these negative forces, or at least minimizing your interactions with them, you can safely consider what needs to be done to get things finished and successfully launched. Put plenty of margin between yourself and the negativity.

DEVELOPING AN INTERNAL COMPASS

The second area to address in terms of innovation is to work toward developing an internal compass. When you focus on innovating, you need to learn to trust yourself and build your own internal sense of direction.

Listen to Your Gut

Innovation is often a quiet process; you need to listen to those ideas whose voices seem the faintest. Write them down so they don't escape your notice.

Over time, as you accumulate these little nuggets, you may begin to see a larger landscape, almost like pieces of a puzzle falling into place. Eventually, you may assemble enough of the puzzle pieces to start seeing the true picture.

Be patient and observant. Don't give up: Success may be just around the corner.

Learn to Trust Yourself

Often your initial gut feel for how to pursue a problem is correct, learn to trust yourself and your instincts. It's simply unlikely that anyone else has your same background, your same style of thinking, your view of a future world. Your perspective literally is as good as anyone else's. Someone else just may be a little more confident in selling her vision.

Listen to the Customer Closely, But Maintain Your Own Vision

You can't just ask customers what they want and then try to give that to them. By the time you get it built, they'll want something new.

—Steve Jobs, Founder of Apple Computer

Most of your customers will be focused on the problems they are currently encountering with respect to the business environment today and with respect to the system capabilities that they deal with today. They will mostly likely be focused on product innovation.

At the same time, your customers may not have contemplated the possibilities of process innovation. Whether you are dealing with internal or external customers, you may encounter some level of resistance in taking on the expense involved in changing what is perceived to be a process that is already working. Dealing with both positioning and paradigm innovation will require you to talk to new customer groups, some of which may not even exist yet, depending on what you perceive to be the new opportunity.

Listen to what your customers say and be open to their ideas for improvements, but continue to search for the underlying problem:

- Why do your customers consider this issue to be a problem or an area for improvement?
- What are they trying to change or reduce?
- Is this an efficiency play?

- Is it a competitive issue?
- Is it a performance issue?
- Is it a core competency issue? Or is it something your customers need, but do not view as a core competency?
- What is driving your customers toward change? Are business conditions changing?

In many respects, your role is to find the story behind the story, similar to what would be done in investigative reporting. You must gather information to formulate a cohesive story, one that will tell you why this is not only a great product today, but where things are heading and how what you are doing will position you in the future to be a market leader in a market that may not exist yet.

Listen to Others (Collaborate)

If you can, look for someone who would make a good partner in your quest for innovation. Occasionally, you may find someone who complements your position and capabilities—someone you can trust, and someone with whom you can communicate effortlessly. Joining together with this individual, you may be able to forge a nearly unstoppable partnership.

Two individuals who are collaborative partners often have a dramatic ability to influence the organization. Such a duo is able to sell the vision, handle the naysayers from multiple perspectives, and openly collaborate to bring visionary ideas to fruition. This leadership team can pull together multiple overlapping projects that are able to pursue an end-state vision and incrementally deliver value to the organization.

Be careful that you don't unnecessarily alienate others in the process of pursuing your vision. In the end, this negative force could severely affect your prospects for success in the future.

Can You Make a Baby Step Today?

The most successful people are those who are good at Plan B.

—James Yorke

Although innovation may, on the surface, appear to be revolutionary, the path to glory is usually a long road marked by failed attempts, corrections, and persistence in pursuing the goal. As you make progress, you may notice marketable side shoots that appear along the way. Don't let your dogged pursuit of your vision prevent you from making money today.

By finding ways to contribute to the financial health of the company today, you can help finance the continued pursuit of the real goals, the real vision. Success begets success. Oddly enough, one of these offshoots could well prove to be the real innovation, the truly revolutionary idea that may light the marketplace on fire.

As executives begin seeing you deliver incremental parts of the vision (laying the bricks of the foundation), you will begin to earn chits (financial dollars in the world of executive trust). This bank account of trust will allow you to gain the space you need so that when the inevitable failures occur, you have the opportunity to recover from them. Capitalizing on these side-stream innovations can help the company gain an early ROI from the innovation and offsets the costs of the investment needed to realize the long-term vision.

No Is Okay for Today: Keep Plugging Along, Because Yes Will Come

When you're the first person whose beliefs are different from what everyone else believes, you're basically saying, "I'm right, and everyone else is wrong." That's a very unpleasant position to be in. It's at once exhilarating and at the same time an invitation to be attacked.

—Larry Ellison, Founder of Oracle

The resources available to support a proposed innovation may be limited at any given time. It is okay for the business, your boss, or other groups to say no. They need to have the opportunity to be successful on their own terms, to put some of the pieces of the puzzle together in their own heads. You may be, in many respects, a maverick in advocating the particular idea you are pursuing. It takes time to get the organizational momentum behind an idea or concept. Because you know the vision you are pursuing, you should be willing to accept the incremental pieces of support that are offered now and that will help shorten the distance between where you want to go compared to where you are today.

Over time, if you are doggedly persistent (not in an irritating way), the effects of your slow, repeated tapping away (pursuit of the idea) will eventually allow you to chisel a foothold and move closer to your end goal. Over time, step by step, you may climb the mountain and end up at your desired destination. Sometimes this path may take years to traverse. Be prepared to stay the course for the long haul, and limit the number of visionary pursuits that you entertain. If your interests are too diverse, you will become diluted in your pursuit and ultimately ineffective at delivering anything. This can put you in a severely demotivated state if you become blocked on too many fronts.

BLENDING ESSENTIAL CONCEPTS

The final consideration when engaging in innovation is to identify existing concepts, discover new concepts, and then blend the two; this intersection between old and new provides fertile ground for the seeds of innovation (see Figure 10-4).

Read, Read, Read

I have no special talent. I am only passionately curious.

—Albert Einstein

I am sure you have heard the axiom that "leaders are readers." In the world of technology, being aware of the trends in both your own industry and adjacent industries can help you develop related solutions. Solutions fomented in other areas can act as a template or design pattern for how to approach a particular problem. This is the approach that Ray Kroc took more than 50 years ago with the McDonald's restaurant chain. The concept of an assembly line was far from new. What was innovative was Kroc's application of this concept to making hamburgers. The end result was that no matter which McDonald's restaurant you visited, you got food that tasted the same every time at a reasonable cost.[3]

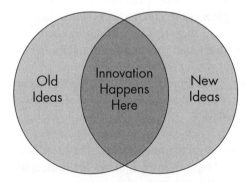

Figure 10-4   Innovation often happens when you take new ideas from other areas and blend them with existing ideas (the core strengths that have enabled your success to date).

---

3.   www.wiley.com/legacy/products/subject/business/forbes/kroc.html

Reading books, blogs, and other materials can help you build a backlog of knowledge that you can readily draw upon whenever you face a challenging problem. It can give you the raw materials—new ideas from the outside to draw in—to apply in an innovative fashion.

Crazy Ideas Help You Discover the Real Boundaries

Mr. Edison, please tell me what laboratory rules you want me to observe.

—M. A. Rosanoff

There ain't no rules around here. We're trying to accomplish somep'n!

—Thomas Edison

When you feel stuck trying to solve a particular problem, brainstorming about all of the approaches that could possibly work can help fuel an innovative approach. Don't be critical of any ideas that are generated; just focus on capturing them. Let yourself be free to explore the universe of possibilities; throw out the rules. Going outside the normal boundaries can help you reframe your context and allow you to see other possibilities—ones that might initially seem a bit outlandish.

Take time to capture all of your ideas. The result may be a great list of seed ideas both for your current problem and potentially for future endeavors.

Once you step outside your normal comfort zone, you have the chance to evaluate a wide range of possible solutions. The real boundaries will become clear as you push the limits. One thing to keep in mind is that the boundaries of yesterday are not necessarily the boundaries that exist today: Technology is always advancing and, as a result, new solutions become available that can act as steppingstones to where you want to go.

Have a Big Vision

The scope of your vision can severely limit the set of alternatives that you consider when trying to solve a particular problem. The vision acts as a natural boundary—a set of fixed assumptions that may be difficult to perceive as a limiting factor.

There may be absolutely incredible business opportunities next door to where you are, but these opportunities may remain imperceptible because they are outside the realm of consideration—they don't match your vision.

In fact, if someone does bring up the opportunity, the idea is likely to be attacked.

When you are setting your vision, think big. Go past the normal boundaries that you can easily see today. Try to stretch far enough so that the vision is something that will require you to grow to attain it now, and will require you to continue to grow well into the future to fully exploit the innovation. This kind of expansive vision will allow you to naturally consider a wide set of alternatives and directions that will provide your company with many new opportunities in the future.

Innovator's Dilemma

One of my favorite books on innovation is *Innovator's Dilemma* by Clayton Christensen. This book focuses on a natural point that most successful companies encounter—that is, when you simply cannot grow your core business any larger. Once you have reached this position, what do you do? Christensen's primary suggestion is to innovate into adjacent markets. The challenge lies in having a thorough understanding of what your core competencies are, what the core competencies of your competitors in the adjacent markets are, and how you can leverage what you are good at to become a dominant player in an adjacent market. This endeavor can be thought of as innovating in the context of your business.

For many problems, looking to other industries (near or far) can help shed light on solutions or patterns that can be used to spark innovative ideas and approaches.

Innovation and Clustering: Getting the Right Group of Things Together

> *The achievement of excellence can only occur if the organization promotes a culture of creative dissatisfaction.*
>
> —Lawrence Miller

Innovation is highly unlikely to be something completely new. Instead, innovation often entails a recombination of existing materials, concepts, or ideas. The trick is to find the magic blend that produces a spark that can be fanned into a flame. Trying different things, making mistakes, and breaking the rules are all a kind of thinking and acceptance that need to be pervasive when you are pursuing innovation.

Take time to consider what you and others have learned from the past:

- What has failed? Why?
- What has worked? Why?
- What were the dreams of yesterday?
- Are these dreams achievable today? Have things progressed in such a manner that the dream is within reach?
- Is the dream still valid?
- Are there different perspectives that you can take regarding the problem? What light does assuming each perspective shed?
- Are there spikes (proofs of concept) that you can undertake to validate your ideas?
- What could you do to better understand the problem?
- How have other industries approached this kind of problem?
- Are there design principles you can leverage?
- Are there analogies that you can draw?

Choose Simplicity

As you begin to peel away the layers from your innovative ideas, take the time to reduce each idea to its simplest elements. Focus on understanding what the true novelty is. This process will accomplish several things:

- It enables you to sell the innovation more easily to executives as you begin to lobby for dollars to fund its development.
- It removes potential barriers that would allow others to dismiss a potentially great new innovation.
- It allows the innovation to spread and be extended. Once your financial stakeholders grok the innovation in its bare form, they will quickly be able to see many potential areas of development and application. At this point, the hook is set, and they can see the road to financial success.
- It may help you uncover multiple interrelated novelties that have their own independent paths to financial success.

Simplification Is the Essence of Intellectual Property

Once you simplify your novel ideas by breaking them down into their smallest cohesive units, you will be well prepared to seek intellectual property protection. When you discuss your invention with a patent attorney, if you have not already started on this simplification, the attorney will begin trying to reduce the innovation to its most fundamental elements and then work to build it back up. The attorney also will help you broaden the potential intellectual property boundaries to which you will want to stake a claim.

Ideally, you want to capture as much intellectual property as you possibly can so that you can effectively keep your competition at bay or at least severely handicapped. When the patent prosecution begins and the patent examiner looks at your invention, if some areas are not deemed patentable, you don't want to lose all of your property rights. Rather, you want to strike out only limited language and maintain the largest claims possible.

Consider the Problem Before the Solution

All too often in architecture, it is easy to rush toward a solution without achieving a solid grasp on the problem. You have your favorite architectural patterns, your favorite design patterns, your favorite technology, your favorite hardware configuration—all hammers looking for a nail to pound on. Your mind tells you that you have the answer at the tip of your tongue, and your ego quickly confirms this premise and inflates when it considers the rapid speed with which yet another dragon was slayed by your mighty arsenal of prebaked solutions (next please). But wait! The dragon seems to be rising . . . Hmm, did I really understand the problem? Possibly not.

When you are faced with a new problem, take time to immerse yourself in the problem and its surrounding issues:

- What is the real problem (not the surface irritation)?
- Why are these issues present? What are the real issues?
- When did they start?
- Have others solved this problem? Does that solution still apply? If not, why not?
- Have you modeled the domain yet?
- Have you had a chance to observe the problem firsthand?
- Have you had a chance to interview users?
- Why do users think this is a problem? How would they solve it? Why haven't they done so?

Once you become one with the problem, the opportunities to introduce innovation become more clearly evident and surface more quickly.

Define the Problem

If you define the problem right, the solution may be readily apparent. Typically, there are only a handful of ways to solve the problem. The challenge is to unwind the assumptions that you hold when first coming to the problem. Take time at the beginning of the process to document which assumptions you are making.

Confirm that the assumptions you are making are, in fact, valid. They may be just historical artifacts of the previous set of projects you have worked on. This phenomenon is one reason why it is helpful to have a constant stream of new blood enter the organization, whether through the use of contractors or new hires. People who are coming from outside the company (and even from outside your department) are not as likely to be encumbered in the tribal knowledge you unconsciously use every day.

Sleep on It

When I was in college and I had a tough math proof to work through, I would study the problem right before I went to bed, and maybe write down some ideas about how to approach it. I was always amazed at the sheer number of times I would wake up in the morning with the proof readily available in my mind; the first thing I would do is get up and write out the proof—problem solved.

The same can be said of innovation. Sometimes, thinking too hard about a problem will nearly guarantee your failure to discover the novelty needed for a breakthrough. Letting your conscious mind focus on other things or sleeping on it can work wonders (see Figure 10-5). Your subconscious, when devoid of all the other distractions in your busy daily life, can focus on nearly infinite permutations in the background (parallel processing at its best) and find the solution you were desperately seeking.

Figure 10-5   Let your mind innovate while you sleep.

According to dream researcher Dr. Deirdre Barrett from Harvard Medical School, dreams are capable of solving problems that we have mental blocks for during our waking hours.[4]

Is It Strategic or Tactical?

Consider the problem that needs to be solved. If all that is needed is a minor modification (a more tactical solution) to an existing system, perhaps no innovation is required. Innovating for the sake of innovation does not provide value. In fact, it may destabilize a working system. Be pragmatic where it makes sense.

BECOMING A INNOVATIVE ARCHITECT

Success is on the far side of failure.

—Thomas Watson, Sr.

The road to becoming an innovative architect begins with the following steps:

- Learning the definition of innovation.
- Establishing margins:
    - Find margin.
    - Innovate at the edge.
    - Take away all of the constraints.
    - Encourage others to think and be open.
    - Be prepared for the naysayers.
    - Minimize your exposure to the naysayers.
- Developing an internal compass:
    - Listen to your gut.
    - Learn to trust yourself.
    - Listen to the customer closely, but maintain your own vision.
    - Listen to others in a collaborative fashion.
    - Learn to take baby steps.
    - Be willing to accept a no today, and continue working toward obtaining a yes in the future.
- Blending essential concepts:
    - Find new concepts by reading, reading, and more reading.
    - Let the crazy ideas in.

---

4. Barrett, D. (1993). The "committee of sleep": A study of dream incubation for problem solving. Dreaming, 3(2), 115–122.

- Have a big vision (and make sure it's big enough).
- Read *Innovator's Dilemma* by Clayton Christensen.
- Cluster the right group of things.
- Put the right mix of concepts together.
- Choose simplicity.
- Understand that intellectual property claims are based on the notion of simplicity.
- Consider the problem before the solution.
- Define the problem.
- Sleep on it; go away a while, and the answer may find you.
- Innovate only when innovation is really needed.

Learning to be an innovative architect can greatly aid you in becoming more effective in your partnerships with the business side of software development. The hardest thing to learn is how to balance your work by blending tactical needs with strategic vision without compromising the integrity of the vision. Effective innovation is more of an art than a fixed recipe for achieving success.

BIBLIOGRAPHY

Amabile, Tereas M.; Brown, John Seely; Craumer, Martha; Drucker, Peter F.; Hadely, Constance N.; Kramer, Steven J.; Levitt, Theodore; Pearson, Andrall E.; Peebles, Ellen; Wolpert, John D. (2003). *Harvard Business Review on the Innovative Enterprise.* Harvard Business School Press.

Christensen, Clayton M.; Raynor, Michael E. (2003). *The Innovator's Solution: Creating and Sustaining Successful Growth.* Harvard Business School Press.

Cooper, Robert G. (2001). *Winning at New Products: Accelerating the Process from Idea to Launch.* Basic Books.

Cornish, Edward. (2004). *Futuring: The Exploration of the Future.* World Future Society.

Hagadorn, Andrew. (2003). *How Breakthroughs Happen: The Surprising Truth About How Companies Innovate.* Harvard Business School Press.

Howard, William G.; Guile, Bruce R. (1992). *Profiting from Innovation: The Report of the Three-Year Study from the National Academy of Engineering.* Free Press.

Kawasaki, Guy (2008). *Reality Check: The Irrelevant Guide to Outsmarting, Outmanaging, and Outmarketing Your Competition.* Portfolio.

Marcus, Alfred. (2005). *Management Strategy: Achieving Sustained Competitive Advantage.* McGraw-Hill.

Marcus, Alfred. (2006). *Winning Moves: Cases in Strategic Management.* Marsh Publications.

Chapter 11

PRAGMATISM

Strategy directly combined with tactical skill is the real killer combo.
Strategy in the absence of tactical engagement is a loser's game.

—Chad Dickerson, CTO at Etsy

Pragmatism is the dose of reality that needs to be mixed into the daily decisions related to architecture. It is easy to dream of architectural ivory towers, elegant designs, and a universe devoid of financial constraints. However, the job of an architect is to hold vision in one hand and reality in the other hand, and to bring them together. The two concepts have a natural resistance to each other—the same way two like-poled magnets repel each other. They can be brought together, but only through force.

This chapter shows how to bring pragmatism to the everyday world of software architecture.

PRAGMATIC ARCHITECTURE DEFINED

Pragmatic architecture is the notion of driving toward an architectural vision (the strategic) while constraining projects to reality (the tactical). That is, project dates, feasibility, financial costs, related project decisions, and leverage capabilities or possibilities all need to be part of the mix in determining the "best" steps for the architectural approach. The key to pragmatic architecture is to manage through scope management, risk management, and communication (see Figure 11-1).

For example, suppose you have a new project proposal that absolutely, positively must ship on a specific date in four months because of a trade show, and there is a limited budget to get it done. The project will deliver a key strategic advantage for your company over your competitors.

The challenge is that three competing architectural approaches are available. The first approach would require the use of some new open-source

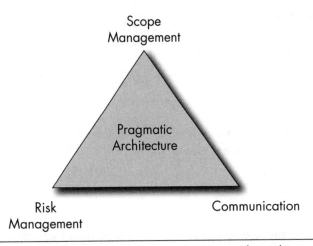

Figure 11-1   Pragmatic architecture means managing the architecture pragmatically through scope management, risk management, and communication.

technologies that your company has no experience with. The second approach would require you to build the solution primarily from the ground up—a mostly greenfield development project, except that it will need to be integrated with several of your legacy systems. The third approach would require you to hack a solution into the current legacy system, and would likely be fragile under heavy use.

You have three days to come up with a final decision; complete cost estimates, resource needs estimates, risks estimates (and their mitigation plans), and key assumptions; and review the proposal with all affected parties. On the fourth day, you will present your plan to the executives, who will be looking to dive deep into any area they like and ensure that the plan of attack is solid.

What do you do (and no, updating your résumé is not an option)?

Read on.

SCOPE MANAGEMENT

The first key area to address in pragmatic architecture is to manage scope. If you take the time to carefully work through the scoping of the project, you will enable success for all of the partners by eliminating risk or bringing awareness to substantive risks, helping the business to prioritize those elements of the project that deliver the highest value for a reasonable cost, and achieving early momentum instead of being entangled in endless analysis.

Work with the Business to Determine Feature Priority

Although you may have your pet priorities for a project (those really cool new technologies or features that are just looking for a project to fund their implementation), you need to consider the business needs to help determine what will really help drive the ROI for this project and allow it to meet or exceed the financial expectations attached to the project. If your pet technologies will truly help the business better meet its needs, then by all means consider them.

Figuring out how to properly sequence the feature development of a particular project can be tricky business. Some infrastructure tasks will likely be needed to implement the flashy new feature that provides the new sales capabilities that will nearly market itself. Taking time to partner with the business can help prioritize the "must have" features and allow you to work through the real dependencies so that the value can be delivered as quickly as possible to the business.

You can think of features as being analogous to a stack of cards (see Figure 11-2). First, you need to prioritize the cards in order of customer value; then, you should plan to execute them in that order. That way, even if you have to stop development mid-project or choose to release the product or service early, you will have delivered the highest-value features and enable the best ROI. The priority cut-off card serves as a checkpoint of whether to continue with the project.

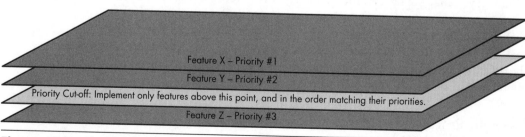

Feature X – Priority #1
Feature Y – Priority #2
Priority Cut-off: Implement only features above this point, and in the order matching their priorities.
Feature Z – Priority #3

Figure 11-2 Think of features as a stack of cards.

One of the key elements in determining feature priority is to avoid saying no (unless the feature is truly unfeasible or not viable with the budget being proposed). This enables the business to manage the project later on and easily expand or reduce the scope of the project in conjunction with critical milestones or releases.

Help Executives Make the Right Decision

When the investment decisions are being made—that is, whether to invest in this project—it is critical to ensure that the executives understand the nature of the decisions that are about to be made and the alternatives that are available. They need to understand what the consequences of the chosen path will be, which limits it will impose upon the future, and what this project will enable.

Deal with Ambiguity

As an architect, you will always have a need for more information to make a more precise decision about the architecture for a particular project. No matter how many details you seek, there will always be a level of ambiguity in the decision-making process.

The challenge is to get to the point where you are comfortable with ambiguity and to develop a sense of when you have sufficient information to make a reasonably calculated approach to allow a project to move forward with known assumptions and risks.

Over time, you will develop a sixth sense for areas you need to investigate more fully or to document as a project assumption or risk.

Sometimes, You Just Need to Start with a Concept

Although you may not have all the answers that you were seeking before you began the journey, there comes a time when you just need to jump off the cliff and go. You may have only a concept in hand and simply need to trust that you will get to the other side. Just make sure that those above you in the organizational hierarchy understand what is known and not known and appreciate the risks associated with the venture.

Use Agile Processes as a Means to Pragmatism

One of the best ways to interject pragmatism into software development is to use agile processes, such as Scrum or Lean. These processes will help you focus on the areas that need to be addressed now, while allowing some ambiguous parts of the project to live in the backlog (list of future development stories) until they need to be addressed as part of an iteration (two-week development cycle) or as part of a spike (time-bounded proof of concept).

The challenge with agile development is to ensure you have some level of focus on the overall roadmap and product releases, thereby ensuring that you continue marching in the direction of your product vision. From an architectural perspective, you also need to ensure that you have stories to deal with the nonfunctional requirements of the system.

Architecture in an agile process still needs to be addressed, of course. Most of the time, however, it just doesn't need to be addressed in its entirety upfront in the project.

RISK MANAGEMENT

The second key area of pragmatic architecture is managing risk. Rarely in a project will a known risk jump out and bite you. Instead, it is always the unknown, undiscovered risk that comes out of nowhere and derails a project. If at all possible, spend time early on in the discovery phase of project estimation to identify, document, and mitigate as many of these potential risks as possible.

Differentiate Between Possible and Feasible

When considering the broad set of possible implementations for an architectural approach, there can be a wide range of feasibility associated with each approach. You need to take the following considerations into account:

- Which resources will implement the system? Do they need any training? Are they familiar with the architectural approach being suggested?
- Has this architectural pattern been implemented previously in your company? In the industry?
- Which architectural spikes may be needed to remove any high-level risks?
- What kind of licensing needs to be procured? Do you know what the costs for this licensing will be? Has anyone worked with the company that is issuing the license? If not, it will be more difficult to bring the tool in. Are you willing to go to bat for this tool if you are challenged by executives? (Choose your battles wisely.)

- Are there special hardware needs? Has your company used this hardware vendor before? Can you execute this project on the cloud?
- Do you understand the nature of scaling the solution (from an application server perspective, from a database perspective, from a network perspective, from a storage device perspective, from a queuing perspective, from a caching perspective, and so on)? Will you need to scale up or scale out?
- Do you have or can you build the appropriate tools that will enable you to monitor the system?
- Have you accounted for any reporting needs?
- Do you understand how to build, deploy, and test the solution?
- Are there any legal or regulatory issues you need to address?
- Do patents or other intellectual property need to be secured or developed for the development work that will occur?
- Does this development effort need any special research and development?
- Do you understand when this project needs to be delivered?
- Are you able to structure the project across multiple organizations in a manner that minimizes coupling between the groups and maximizes cohesion within the groups?
- Do you understand the projected ROI for this project and the elements that will enable this ROI to be delivered? (What promises are being made to the field when this product gets delivered? Can you deliver on those promises?)
- Which alternatives have you considered? Why were some rejected?
- Which future projects are in the pipeline that will build upon this project as strategic infrastructure?
- How does this project align with the company's strategic long-term goals?
- Does the project need to interact with any key software packages?
- Do any key software interfaces need to be implemented?
- Do any key data exchange formats need to be handled?
- Can you contemplate at least one reasonable design and implementation approach?
- Do you understand key alternatives? (If some aspect of the project fundamentally fails, what are the alternatives—do you have a good Plan B?) When during the project does a particular path need to be determined?

One way to increase the feasibility of a project is to minimize the number of new things you are injecting into the organization or to sequence the changes such that you allow your project to incorporate the changes in a stable manner. Bringing in new things is fun, but trying to get them operationalized is nearly always a challenge. Choose your battles carefully. Understand the nature of the delivery dates related to your ability to ingest the changes.

Another aspect of addressing feasibility is to properly set expectations of all key stakeholders in terms of assumptions, risks, financial costs, and alternatives.

You may not be able to answer all the questions, but attempting to do so will help you sort out whether the approach you suggest is feasible within your organization.

Ask Yourself Key Questions About Every Decision

With every decision you make, assess the risk impact of that decision (see Figure 11-3).

To help determine this impact, consider the following questions:

- What are the operational implications of this decision?
- What are the hardware implications of this decision?
- What are the training implications of this decision?
- What are the maintenance cost implications of this decision?
- Have any key architectural tenets been broken by this decision?
- What is the developmental cost of this decision?
- Will the decision enable the project to meet its delivery dates faster?
- Will the quality of the project be affected materially?
- Are all key stakeholders committed to this change? If not, why not?

Increased Risk

Decreased Risk

Figure 11-3 What is the risk impact of the decision you are about to make? Are you and the team really willing to take on the change necessitated by a risk?

Deal with Likely Risks

The number of risks associated with a project has the potential to be large. Although these risks may need some minimal amount of think time, the areas you want to concentrate on are the real risks. These are the risks that have a likely chance of happening—such as a new technology failing to deliver as planned, a dependent project failing to deliver, or a financial challenge that requires you to do with less.

These likely risks and your ability to plan how to address them and which alternatives must be considered if and when they happen will dramatically affect your ability to succeed on a regular basis. If you are able to deliver on your promises even under dire circumstances, you will gain the reputation you need to be able to advance further up in the organization. (When everything seems to go right, don't worry: Murphy's Law is usually just around the corner waiting to add adventure to your life in new and exciting ways.)

Architectural Spikes

When key decisions need to be made with respect to the feasibility of a particular architectural approach, take the time to do a time-bounded architectural spike (proof of concept). This exercise can help you gain insight into the appropriate route to take. To ensure a successful spike, follow these guidelines:

- Place time boundaries on the investigation.
- Understand the key elements that require investigation.
- Avoid implementing a complete solution.
- Avoid allowing the architectural spike to turn into the real solution (make it ugly).
- Document your results and recommendations. (Other groups will find this information helpful.)
- Get the right resources on the architectural spike—those people who can dive into murky, uncharted waters and get tasks done with minimal help.

Work with Operations to Determine Efficiency

The operational costs of a particular project can sink its chances of being implemented, kill it after it has been launched, or divert precious resources to putting fingers in a dam that is leaking. Involving those personnel who deal with the operational side of software development early on in the project development life cycle can help minimize the operational costs once the project has gone into production.

These resources will have insights into which types of information they need to access to deal with customers, such as customer complaints, customer change requests, customer billing, and customer delivery alternatives. They may have insights into internal processes as well. Learn how they are accustomed to processing information and identify the types of special access, overrides, reprocessing, or other high-priority needs they have.

Observe Other Projects to Determine What Is Acceptable to Sacrifice

When things go wrong for a project (and they will), be prepared to throw things overboard (not everything is of equal value). You need to work with the business to determine which features are really nice to have (everything upfront is a "must have") and which strategic aspects of the project will have to wait for another day. Identify whether automated parts of the process can be manually done (at least for a while); this is the point when the project gets real—when all of the lofty goals and aspirations turn toward getting the end result out the door.

As other projects reach this phase, watch and observe what happens. Which compromises are considered acceptable, which compromises are considered not acceptable, and which projects end up succeeding or failing? This inside information is essential to have at your disposal when your project hits some roadblocks and alternatives need to be pursued.

COMMUNICATION

The third key area of pragmatic architecture is bringing clarity to communication. Unless you focus on clear, consistent, and continuous communication, all of your great architectural efforts may quickly be swept away by ineffective or absent communication. Any communication gap will nearly always be filled in by others, and often in ways that do not flatter architects. Stay on top of the communication process, even when you are extraordinarily busy (see Figure 11-4).

Document Agreed-Upon Resolutions

A certain amount of flexibility is needed during the implementation of a project. You need to clearly communicate in which areas of the project there is some flexibility in terms of approach or features.

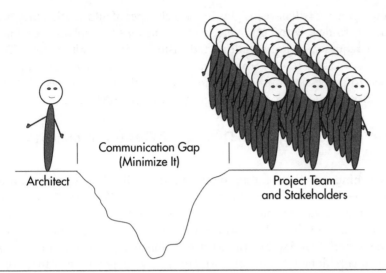

Figure 11-4   When it comes to communication, you cannot possibly over-communicate. Seek to communicate clearly, consistently, and continuously. It will make your life and the lives of everyone on the team go more smoothly and efficiently.

Once a decision (a commitment) has been made for a particular path, you need to enforce it by following through with the decision. Sometimes, the business may be a bit tentative or unsure of what the right answer is or may not have done the necessary field studies to understand certain customer nuances. If possible, try to understand the nature of where changes may be required, and build flexibility into the designs to accommodate these changes if it is not overly expensive. Otherwise, seek to hold off on implementing new features until customer feedback is available.

Unfortunately, when software is being built, only a limited amount of variability and flexibility can be realized. Indecisiveness that leads to significant rework will burn precious development dollars and needs to be kept to a minimum.

Take the time to document decisions along the way. Ensure that the decision log is properly distributed so that there are no surprises. The key to success is proper expectations setting and transparency.

Present Multiple Alternatives and Make a Recommendation

Whenever you need to present alternatives as part of making a decision, whether to executives, business partners, or even your kids, your ability to clearly articulate which options are available and which option you would recommend will produce a great starting point for a conversation.

Don't be afraid to recommend the solution you want; you will often get what you wish for. Be willing to defend your choice and show that you have really thought through the decision, but be supportive of others who choose options that don't match your recommendation.

If someone does choose an option that you did not recommend, move forward and own the decision as if you made it. At the same time, make sure the decision maker understands the consequences of that decision (e.g., delays, cost).

Use Transparency to Level Expectations

When decisions need to be made, lay the full set of facts on the table (full transparency), even when doing so is not to your advantage. Such transparency will help build trust. Later, when things go well, there will be a sense of partnership that emerges from working through the problems, versus creating an adversarial environment where some parties feel they were not treated well and did not have all the known information up front for making the decision. In the latter case, when the next project comes along, the other side will be much more cautious when working with you and the trust factor will be minimal.

If you need to deliver bad news about a project, ensure that everyone on the team knows about it before the information is raised to the executive level. You should strive for a policy of no surprises. This may not always be possible, but try to make it the norm.

Try to communicate any new major risks as quickly as you can to the sponsoring executives for a project. If the risks are significant, executives need to be involved early on to help properly communicate the information to the rest of the organization and formulate the best approach for minimizing the risk.

Develop Rules of Thumb for Sizing Projects

Over time, you will begin to notice certain patterns with respect to sizing projects. Often, these patterns can be codified into rules of thumb for estimating how big the project will be and how many resources (people or hardware) will be needed.

The rule of thumb may be something to the effect that X number of concurrent users require Y number of servers for a particular type of user interface. Ideally, this information will be based on real stress or load tests.

This type of information can become part of the tribal knowledge for addressing new projects. The challenge is to understand which constraints apply with the rule of thumb so that you don't use it when the assumptions don't hold.

BECOMING A PRAGMATIC ARCHITECT

The road to becoming a pragmatic architect begins with the following steps:

- Become familiar with the notion of pragmatic architecture.
- Scope management:
    - Work with the business to determine feature priority.
    - Help executives to make the right decisions.
    - Learn to deal with ambiguity.
    - Start sometimes with only a concept.
    - Use agile processes.
- Risk management:
    - Differentiate between possible and feasible.
    - Ask yourself key questions surrounding every decision.
    - Deal with likely risks.
    - Use architectural spikes.
    - Work with operations personnel to determine efficiency.
    - Observe what is acceptable to sacrifice.
- Communication:
    - Document agreed-upon resolutions.
    - Present multiple alternatives and make a recommendation.
    - Use transparency to level expectations.
    - Develop rules of thumb.

Learning to be a pragmatic architect can sap some of the fun from the honeymoon phase of a project, but delivering project after project on time and on budget in the end is very rewarding. It will help you move up in your career and it will give you a great sense of accomplishment to see the real customer value being delivered.

BIBLIOGRAPHY

Burnett, Mark. (2001). *Dare to Succeed: How to Survive and Thrive in the Game of Life.* Hyperion.

Cathy, S. Truett. (1989). *It's Easier to Succeed Than to Fail.* Thomas Nelson Publishers.

Joyner, Mark. (2007). *Simpleology: The Simple Science of Getting What You Want.* Wiley.

Magee, David. (2004). *Ford Tough: Bill Ford and the Battle to Rebuild America's Automaker.* Wiley.

Maxwell, John C. (1998). *The 21 Irrefutable Laws of Leadership: Follow Them and People Will Follow.* Thomas Nelson.

Salka, John. (2004). *First In, Last Out: Leadership Lessons from the New York Fire Department.* Portfolio.

Swensen, Richard A. (1992). *Margin: Restoring Emotional, Physical, Financial, and Time Reserves to Overloaded Lives.* NAVPRESS.

Chapter 12

VISION

If you want to be happy, set a goal that commands your thoughts, liberates your energy, and inspires your hopes.

—Andrew Carnegie

The greatest danger for most of us is not that our aim is too high and we miss it, but that it is too low and we reach it.

—Michelangelo

You cannot depend on your eyes when your imagination is out of focus.

—Mark Twain

Have you ever been on a project or worked at a company that lacked vision? It simply lacked that compelling idea that drew everything together, and its absence resulted in a dearth of focused and directed effort. If you haven't, you are lucky. If you have, you know the challenges that are faced by a project or company that meanders. It feels as if you are caught churning in the surf with no way out. It's not fun, and it saps your energy.

Vision is invisible. Although you can't see it, you know when it's present. You can feel it; it surrounds you and permeates everything. Vision drives how you think, what you do, how you do it, your energy level, and your sense of purpose.

Vision is a dance with the future.

This chapter focuses on how vision and strategy can be used as a guiding force in the world of architecture.

VISION DEFINED

Vision is a mental image or concept representing an ideal end state that can be used as a guide for focusing and aligning everything that surrounds what you seek to accomplish.

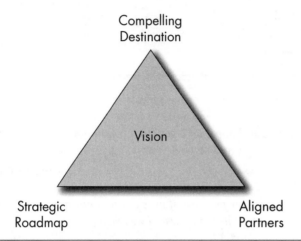

Figure 12-1   Key elements of establishing your vision

Vision requires a compelling destination, a strategic roadmap, and aligned partners to move it from simply being a dream to being a mission with force (see Figure 12-1).

FINDING AND ESTABLISHING A COMPELLING DESTINATION

This section focuses on key aspects of finding and establishing a compelling destination for your vision. These key aspects include discovering your vision, crafting a compelling story around your vision, and overcoming roadblocks.

Discovering Your Vision

The future belongs to those who see possibilities before they become obvious.

—John Sculley, Former CEO of Pepsi and Apple Computer

Don't underestimate the power of a vision. McDonald's founder, Ray Kroc, pictured his empire long before it existed, and he saw how to get there. He invented the company motto—"Quality, service, cleanliness, and value"—and kept repeating it to employees for the rest of his life.

—Kenneth Labich[1]

---

1.   www.leadershipnow.com/visionquotes.html

Vision usually begins as a faint glimmer, a sparkle off in the distance that for some reason grabs your attention. Sometimes it does not seem to exist at all, but you have a sense that you need to go somewhere, although you may not have any idea where that may be. To help jumpstart the vision discovery process, consider the following questions and activities (see Figure 12-2):

- Write down or sketch any of the ideas that have been bouncing around in your head. Don't worry if they are right or wrong—just start capturing them. The key is to begin brainstorming and documenting ideas so as to start filling out more detail around the beginning of your vision. Refinement will happen later.
- Can you draw some diagrams that capture the essence of your thoughts?
- Is there a person or small group of people who share your interest in this matter? If so, can they join you in the brainstorming of ideas around the vision? Collaborating with others will likely enable you to come up with a much crisper image of the future end state, especially if the people with whom you are working share your passion and a sense of trust.
- Do you see any patterns beginning to emerge? If so, what are they?
- What grabs your attention about this particular matter?
- Is the vision too concrete, or does it have some level of ambiguity?
- Is there a particular problem you are trying to solve? Why does it need to be solved?
- Is there a particular customer base you are trying to thrill? Is this effort related to the customer base you have today, or are you trying to move into an adjacent market?
- Is your vision related to the overall company vision? If so, how is it the same? How is it different? Aligning your vision to an overall company direction can help sell it later.
- Is your vision related to the product market space or technology space? The areas to which vision can be applied may have many different facets: organizational structure (e.g., human, software, hardware, pricing), product suites, product features, product pricing, product integration capabilities, product sales channels, customer segmentation, software development processes, software construction, middleware and its configuration, hardware and its configuration, and more. Each facet has the potential to inspire an independent vision and its own associated strategies for how to pursue fulfilling it.

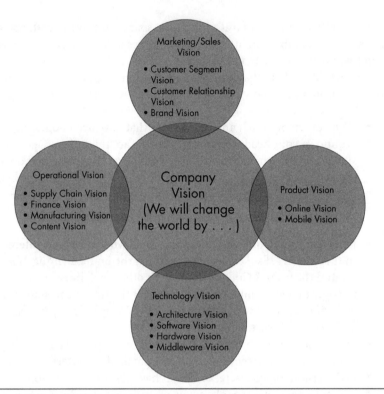

Figure 12-2   Vision within a company is multifaceted, so it's important to know which vision you are pursuing.

The most important aspect of discovering vision is just to start. Take time to brainstorm, include others when appropriate, and give it time to evolve and grow. Make sure you capture the surrounding ideas in some permanent form; this helps capture the evolution; otherwise, ideas may get lost along the way.

Crafting a Compelling Story from Vague Facts

Vision is the art of seeing the invisible.

—Jonathan Swift

Developing a vision is hard work. You need to be able to take what appear to be independent facts and insights and weave them together into a compelling story. These insights and facts usually begin to emerge from having immersed yourself in a particular area that you are passionate about.

As you dive deeper and deeper into the area, you begin to see nuances that were not apparent to you before. Gradually, these nuances begin to coalesce in your mind until you have a better sense of the thing that is drawing your attention to it. As you look to solve particular problems, your sense of what could be becomes stronger and stronger.

You begin to have a sense of being at the edge; the notions surrounding the concept begin to solidify, and a vision appears. Usually at this point, you nearly get goose bumps thinking about arriving at your newfound destination. You have a level of passion and interest that are nearly overwhelming.

Your compelling story is begging to emerge. When you reach this point, consider the following questions:

- Do emerging trends within the industry relate to your vision? Consider looking at analyses like the Gartner hype cycles. Being able to compare and contrast your vision with industry trends will help make it a more compelling story.
- What do you see as the big opportunities? What are the major risks?
- Have you started putting together a presentation or white paper that captures and organizes your ideas and tells the compelling story?

Documenting this information will give others the context they need to see the possibilities surrounding the vision and potentially add insights that may bring more clarity to the overall vision. With their input, the vision will slowly begin to unveil itself, clarity is added, and a compelling story begins to emerge.

Overcoming Roadblocks

You may encounter challenges in trying to formulate a vision; sometimes it seems as if there are distractions at nearly every corner. If things don't begin to coalesce, your initial passion—your sense of being onto something truly great—may have cooled. When you begin to hit these types of roadblocks, contemplate the following questions:

- What are the specific roadblocks that you are encountering?
- Are these roadblocks in any way related to the past? If so, in which way? Has your company encountered previous challenges in this area?
- Are there parts of the vision that you are avoiding?
- Are there ways to vet the ideas with a company or industry expert who may be able to shed light on alternative approaches to move you past the roadblock?

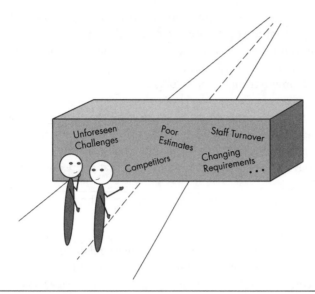

Figure 12-3   Be prepared to encounter roadblocks and be prepared to listen to others.

- How can you remove or move around the roadblocks? What changes need to be made to eliminate the roadblocks?
- Are there people who could potentially be your mentors in developing your vision? Their years of experience may help you quickly overcome roadblocks or help you see roadblocks that are present, but not visible to you.

Be aware of roadblocks as they emerge and prioritize their importance against the overall goals you are trying to achieve (see Figure 12-3). If and when you begin to address these roadblocks, frame them as problems to be solved. This approach will naturally engage your solution-finding instincts instead of focusing on assigning blame. It also begins to give any roadblocks the necessary attention needed to remove or ignore them.

DEVELOPING AND ESTABLISHING A STRATEGIC ROADMAP

After establishing a vision with a compelling destination full of context to draw others in, the next step is to formulate a roadmap for how to get from where you are today to where you want to be. This section focuses on key aspects of developing and establishing a strategic roadmap.

Mapping the Route to Your Vision

Vision without execution is hallucination.

—Thomas Edison

When you start looking at the vision and considering ways to implement it, the thought of getting there may overwhelm you. The best way to eat the proverbial elephant is to take one bite at a time.

To take things step by step, build a roadmap to your ideal end state. Even if it proves to be inaccurate, you can adjust it once you have more and better information (see Figure 12-4).

To start building a roadmap, consider the following questions:

- How big is your vision? Will it take nine months to implement or nine years? With smaller visions, it is easier to see how to get to the end from the starting point. By comparison, larger visions are likely to be ambiguous and the exact steps to get there may be unclear. Larger visions allow you and your organization to grow as the implementation effort gains momentum. If this vision is too small, you can quickly and easily achieve it; as a result, you will likely lose the momentum you worked so hard to establish.
- Are there three to five natural steps or progressions that can be used as the beginnings of a vision roadmap?

Figure 12-4 Build a roadmap to your ideal end state.

- Are there foundational steps that are truly prerequisites and need to be completed before other steps can begin? If so, make sure these steps are dealt with early on.
- Are some steps easier to achieve? If so, can you accomplish some of them earlier in the sequence? Having some early successes may provide enough momentum to propel you through more difficult stages later on, when the trip is more challenging.
- Are some steps so vague that they require additional research and investigations to fully understand? Are these steps likely to stretch the organization in a significant way? Sequence these steps toward the end of the implementation process. This allows you more time to bring them into focus before you get there.
- Can you describe the steps in a relatively short manner?
- Can you construct a one-page diagram that captures the essence of the roadmap?

Getting your vision laid out on paper may initially seem deflating, as it highlights the arduous path to glory, but it will be an essential tool for bringing others on board.

Establishing Strategies to Support the Vision

As you prepare to journey down the path of your roadmap to your destination, you need to be prepared with strategies that can help further guide and shape your decisions. These strategies need to be well known and publicly available to the teams that will be working on the projects associated with your vision. The strategies will allow others to make decisions that are in alignment with what you would have chosen even when you are absent.

In developing strategies, consider the following questions related to your vision:

- What are the key drivers?
- Which patterns do you want to repeat and weave through your vision, strategy, and design?
- Is the vision evolving? If so, how? What effects will the evolution have on your strategies?
- Are there enabling technologies that need development?
- Is open-source adoption a key element of your plan?
- Are there any trade secrets?
- Are there any patents you want to pursue to help secure the legal property rights surrounding any of your innovations?

- Do you need to align your strategies with the strategies of others within the company?
- Do you have the skill set needed to realize your vision? Do you need to hire, train, or contract with individuals?

Developing and establishing strategies in support of your vision can help maintain the constancy of that vision even when you are not around. It can also help increase your return on investment by providing a more consistent approach as technologies are selected and operationalized.

ESTABLISHING ALIGNED PARTNERS

This section focuses on three important aspects of bringing a vision to life: alignment, partnership, and funding. These aspects are analogous to good soil, plenty of sunshine, and nutrient-filled water: If you don't have these resources, your vision will wither and die, so be prepared and seek them early.

Vision Requires Alignment

As your vision expands its boundaries and the number of people involved grows, aligning the steps of the roadmap to the other parties' concerns will help sell your vision. As this expansion occurs, consider the following:

- Where are your customers (internal or external) trying to go?
- What are your customers (internal or external) willing to pay for?

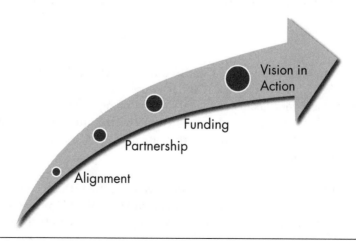

Figure 12-5 Alignment, partnership, and funding bring a vision to life.

- Where is the industry trying to go? Where is your company trying to go?
- Are there trends within the industry or your company with which you can align your vision? Aligning with larger trends is like catching a rising tide; it will naturally help raise your boat.
- What is the current level of commitment within your organization toward your vision? Do you have executive support?
- Who are the caretakers of your company's or division's vision? What are their thoughts surrounding your vision? You need to seek alignment from these key individuals, as they will likely influence your ability to receive funding.
- Are there areas that are out of alignment? If so, are there parts of the vision that you can postpone or change in a manner that will remove the obstacles that are causing the misalignment?
- Is your current vision relevant to the marketplace (internal or external) or is it out-of-date? If it has aged, which aspects of the marketplace have shifted? Which aspects of your customers have shifted? Which aspects of the technology have shifted? You need to know where you are at before you can determine which course adjustments are needed to get you to where you want to be.

Answering these questions and making the necessary adjustments to your vision will help you craft the holistic sales message you need to begin drawing everyone into alignment toward your vision.

Vision Requires Key Stakeholders

Our success has really been based on partnerships from the very beginning.

—Bill Gates, Founder of Microsoft

From an architecture perspective, architects rarely truly own anything. Instead, the only lever they apply for accomplishing anything is the establishment of a vision. That is, they craft a convincing story/vision surrounding the product capabilities, development activities, and construction of a particular project or program, and they are able to infuse that vision into the technology organization.

This reality of a vision can be significantly magnified if partnerships can be forged with key stakeholders. These stakeholders often have the political influence and investment dollars necessary to make a vision truly possible.

They also often have the envisioning skills necessary to help shape and craft the story behind the vision in a manner that enables it to be sold throughout the organization.

This kind of partnership causes many of the roadblocks typically encountered to simply vanish. It also creates a powerhouse of consecutive projects that are able to incrementally build the strategic infrastructure necessary for delivering on the vision.

The challenge is to find and partner with the key individuals within your company or within the industry who can help bring the necessary support and funding you need to move forward.

Vision Requires Funding

Although the exploratory parts of envisioning are fun, the venture will go nowhere if it does not have financial support. If you have drawn in key stakeholders, you may have the political support necessary to put your vision into action. You need to understand the following issues:

- Who needs to approve your vision to gain financial support?
- How big of a market (inside or outside of the company) is there for your vision?
- Are you in a position to seek funding? If not, who can you partner with to seek funding?
- What business value will be reached by pursuing your vision? What is the return on investment?
- What is the minimum amount of investment required to seed your vision?
- Can you obtain funding from multiple sources to support your vision?
- What is the time horizon for completing your vision? For completing the first step in your roadmap?
- What are comparable companies investing in similar ventures? This information may not be publicly available, but you may be able to obtain related information that gives you a sense of the level of investment or talk to industry experts who can quantify this issue.

Obtaining the necessary funding may be the hardest step in turning your vision into a reality. It will require persistence, salesmanship, detailed working knowledge, and enthusiastic passion to get the funds you need.

Remember that those providing the funding will naturally have a "what's in it for me" motivation. To address this issue, be prepared with an explanation of how the company will benefit, including financially, possibly with some estimated ROI figures to back up the request.

VISION IN PRACTICE

This section presents practical ways that vision can be utilized in the everyday world of architecture.

Using Vision to Increase ROI as a Strategy

> *You've got to think about big things while you're doing small things, so that all the small things go in the right direction.*
>
> —Alvin Toffler

> *If you want to build a ship, don't herd people together to collect wood and don't assign them tasks and work, but rather teach them to long for the endless immensity of the sea.*
>
> —Antoine de Saint-Exupery[2]

Over time, the vision may change, but there remains an immense value in synchronizing the vision across multiple projects to build toward an ideal future state. This synchronization can help build the infrastructure needed to support future projects—projects that might otherwise not be considered viable due to their low ROI.

Focusing on vision helps reduce the short-term focus that many projects have in simply trying to meet a current date. If shortcuts need to be taken, you have a measuring stick with which to determine their long-term impacts. As a result, you can choose to take shortcuts in areas that do not fundamentally prevent you from moving toward your strategic vision.

The synergizing of projects also helps to establish a strategic heartbeat throughout the organization, which will implicitly drive others to begin looking for ways to align their work with the vision. The vision in many respects may begin to take on a life of its own, with micro-level alignments

---

2. www.leadershipnow.com/visionquotes.html

occurring simply due to the shared knowledge. This process helps reduce the overall costs of achieving the vision. Eventually, you may begin to hear people repeat messages to you that you helped initially evangelize.

Using Vision to Instill a Sense of Purpose

When there is no vision, the people perish.

—Proverbs 29:18

When you have vision, it affects your attitude. Your attitude is optimistic rather than pessimistic.

—Charles R. Swindoll

Have you ever been on a project that lacked vision and marched colorlessly toward what appeared to be a random delivery date, but was nonetheless driven hard by management? People fell by the wayside, but the march continued; even after important features dropped, the march continued . . . Eventually, you reached the end state—the project was delivered—but there was no pride in what had been built; everyone was simply happy to move on to something else.

Contrast this with a project where there is clarity of vision—a promised land where revenue growth flows freely and customers are standing in line just hoping to use your product. The ability to motivate and self-motivate on projects with this kind of exciting vision is easy. There is a sense of purpose. When the project delivers its final product or service, everyone is sad that it has ended; there is a sense of loss.

The actual difference between these two projects may not be all that great. The key element is that one has a shared vision, while the other does not.

Finding a vision is one way to give people in an organization a sense of purpose. It helps energize them for tackling the work that needs to be done, and it helps align the organization so that employees naturally march in the same direction. Vision helps draw the best people to your organization. It helps you deliver your products and services faster and cheaper with each incremental step forward.

The converse is also true: If the leadership is devoid of vision, the organiza-tion will likely wither and die.

Applying Vision During Project Estimation

The whole world steps aside for the man who knows where he is going.

—Anonymous

When you begin estimating large projects or programs, look for ways to draw in vision—the compelling destination or concept that will focus the energies of the organization. Explicating the vision during the estimating phase can help give people a sense of what the expectations are and what they are aligning to, and can help produce a cohesive project estimate.

When creating project estimates, to get people aligned, consider develop-ing a one-slide "vision document" that shows the vision and the path to get there in a pictorial fashion. This picture will help clarify team members' thinking, establish a framework for the estimating team to hang their ideas off of, and establish a common vocabulary for the project.

As the project begins, the pictorial vision will encourage the team to estab-lish the early goals of the development effort as the roadmap for delivering functionality is formulated. The vision will naturally weave itself through the disparate thinking that occurs within each part of the organization and help align current and future deliverables.

Developing a Spending Envelope (Scoping the Vision)

During the estimation of a project, help the project manager put a spending envelope around the project. Many companies will allow as much as 10% variance on overall project costs before they require a formal revision of the project estimation.

A spending envelope applied to each phase of a roadmap will assist you in determining when a more tactical approach (a well-known alternative) needs to be pursued in favor of a strategic solution. This doesn't mean the strategic solution will not be addressed in the future; rather, it may simply mean that it is not appropriate for today.

BECOMING AN ARCHITECT WITH VISION

The road to becoming an architect with vision begins with the following steps:

- Understanding the definition of vision.
- Finding and establishing a compelling destination:
  - Discover your vision.
  - Craft a compelling story from vague facts.
  - Overcome roadblocks.
- Developing and establishing a strategic roadmap:
  - Map the route to your vision.
  - Establish strategies to support your vision.
- Establishing aligned partners:
  - Vision requires alignment.
  - Vision requires key stakeholders.
  - Vision requires funding.
- Vision in practice:
  - Use vision to increase ROI as a strategy.
  - Use vision to instill a sense of purpose.
  - Apply vision during project estimation to gain alignment.
  - Develop a spending envelope to drive tactical versus strategic solutions.

Learning to be an architect with vision can help direct the suite of projects that you oversee so that they flourish and feed into the vision. By taking the time to go above and beyond your normal architectural duties, and by striving to develop an architectural vision that aligns with the business you work for, you boost your career potential and launch yourself on an exciting journey.

BIBLIOGRAPHY

Cornish, Edward. (2004). *Futuring: The Exploration of the Future.* World Future Society.

Doucet, Gary; Gotze, John; Saha, Pallab; Bernard, Scott. (2009). *Coherency Management: Architecting the Enterprise for Alignment, Agility and Assurance.* Author House.

Kilts, James M.; Mandfredi, John F.; Lorber, Rober. (2007). *Doing What Matters: How to Get Results That Make a Difference—The Revolutionary Old-Fashioned Approach* [Audio CD]. Random House Audio.

Marcus, Alfred. (2005). *Management Strategy: Achieving Sustained Competitive Advantage.* McGraw-Hill.

Marcus, Alfred. (2006). *Winning Moves: Cases in Strategic Management.* Marsh Publications.

Millet, Stephen M.; Honton, Edward J. (1991). *A Manager's Guide to Technology Forecasting and Strategy Analysis Methods.* Battelle Press.

Schmitt, Bernd H. (2008). *Big Think Strategy: How to Leverage Bold Ideas and Leave Small Thinking Behind (Your Coach in a Box)* [Audio CD]. Your Coach Digital.

INDEX

243

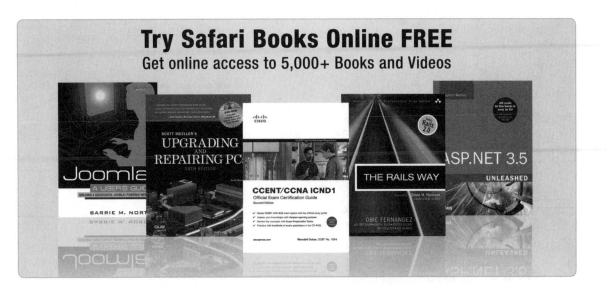

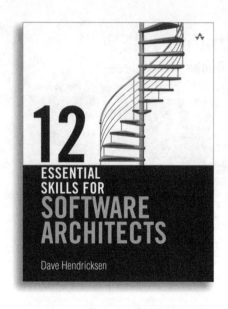

FREE Online Edition

Your purchase of **12 Essential Skills for Software Architects** includes access to a free online edition for 45 days through the Safari Books Online subscription service. Nearly every Addison-Wesley Professional book is available online through Safari Books Online, along with more than 5,000 other technical books and videos from publishers such as Cisco Press, Exam Cram, IBM Press, O'Reilly, Prentice Hall, Que, and Sams.

SAFARI BOOKS ONLINE allows you to search for a specific answer, cut and paste code, download chapters, and stay current with emerging technologies.

Activate your FREE Online Edition at www.informit.com/safarifree

> **STEP 1:** Enter the coupon code: ZYMJGWH.

> **STEP 2:** New Safari users, complete the brief registration form.
> Safari subscribers, just log in.

If you have difficulty registering on Safari or accessing the online edition, please e-mail customer-service@safaribooksonline.com